THE RED DEVILS
QUIZ BOOK

THE RED DEVILS QUIZ BOOK

JOHN DT WHITE

APEX PUBLISHING LTD

First published in 2006, updated and reprinted in 2008 by
Apex Publishing Ltd
PO Box 7086, Clacton on Sea, Essex, CO15 5WN, England

www.apexpublishing.co.uk

British Library Cataloguing-in-Publication Data
A catalogue record for this book
is available from the British Library

ISBN 1-904444-39-3   978-1-904444-39-8

Typeset in 10.5pt Times New Roman

Production Manager: Chris Cowlin

Cover Design: Siobhan Smith

Printed and bound in Great Britain

This book is dedicated to my wife, Janice, and to our two sons,
Marc & Paul and to EVERY single United fan.
And on a final note, Keano thanks for the memories
and Bestie, we miss you.

FOREWORD

It is with great pleasure that I write the Foreword to John's "*The Red Devils Quiz Book*". I can't honestly admit to knowing all of the answers to the Questions but like me I'm sure you will find it enjoyable attempting them. I find myself tackling the questions in between training. I take great delight asking the players the questions I couldn't get right. I love seeing their faces grimace when I tell them the answer. But, nobody likes a know-all do they?

When you open this book you will find it difficult to put it down. And what's more John and Apex Publishing Limited have kindly agreed to donate £1 from every copy sold to the 'George Best's Liver Research Appeal'.

So in closing I hope you find this book as enjoyable as I did and on behalf of myself and all the players, thank you for your loyal support.

Alex Ferguson

Sir Alex Ferguson CBE

INTRODUCTION

I would like to begin with thanking the Boss for writing the Foreword for my Book. I don't need to tell any Red out there just how much of an honour and privilege it is for me to have Sir Alex Ferguson support what I have done but what is even more remarkable is that this is the second time the Boss has written a Foreword to a book for me. The man knows what I think of him - he is a Genius, the Master, the Greatest Football Manager of all time but above all else, he is a True Gentleman.

I would also like to thank all of those people who said such nice things about this Book - Sir Bobby Charlton, Paddy Crerand, Rio Ferdinand, David Gill, Mark Hughes, Denis Law, Wilf McGuinness, Barry Moorhouse, Phil Neville, Mikael Silvestre and many more. It is a great compliment to have past and present Manchester United players appreciate my work and I am deeply honoured with their individual contributions. My thanks must also go to Paul Higson at **www.red11.org** and to Jonathan McCleery at **www.manutdzone.com**. These two guys were extremely helpful when it came to me making my mind up over a particular fact, statistic or an answer to a Quiz question. And lastly, but certainly not least, I would like to thank Frankie 'Dodger' Dodds for the superb artwork and design of the cover.

I wrote this Book for ALL REDS out there regardless of religion or race because we are all part of the one family - MANCHESTER UNITED. I am proud to be a Manchester United fan and I enjoy nothing better than the ABUs having a pop at us when they think we are down and on the way out. True to form we always ram their jibes right back down their throats because as the song says "For Man Utd will never die".

I have a huge sticker on the rear window of my car that reads: "SUPPORT MU, EAT FOOTBALL, DRINK FOOTBALL, SLEEP FOOTBALL, HATE EVERYONE". I would say that just about sums me up. No seriously, I love my family and I do have friends but as regards the other statements, I cannot argue with any of them. There is not a single day of my life that passes by that I do not think of United.

Keep The Red Flag Flying & Come On United!

John "Chalkie" White

LEGEND - ERIC CANTONA - 1

1. What was the first trophy Eric won with United?

2. From what club did United sign Eric?

3. What was Eric's last season at Old Trafford?

4. What City did Alex Ferguson follow Eric to in 1995 when it was believed Eric was about to turn his back on English football?

5. Eric made his United debut as a substitute in December 1992. Can you recall the opposition that day?

6. Name the French club where Eric began his professional career.

7. Eric took a total of 19 penalties for Manchester United. How many times did he find the back of the net from the spot?

8. True of False, Eric scored on his international debut for France?

9. In what competition did he score a hat-trick in August 1992?

10. Eric starred in a film entitled "Le Bonheur". In it he played a sportsman but can you name the sport?

THE BUSBY BABES

11. In what season did United win their first FA Youth Cup?

12. How many FA Youth Cups did the Busby Babes win during the 1950's?

13. What was United's lowest league position during the 1950's?

14. How many First Division Championships did The Reds win during the 1950's?

15. Against which Welsh club did Duncan Edwards make his debut for the Reds?

16. How many of their remaining 14 league games did United win after the Munich Air Disaster?

17. The Babes biggest league win of the 1956-1957 season was a 6-1 home win on 12 January 1957. Can you name the unlucky visitors?

18. By how many points did the Babes win the 1955-1956 First Division Championship 11, 13 or 15?

19. Apart from the FA Youth Cup, what other major Youth Cup did the Babes win in 1954?

20. In the 1958-1959 season United equalled the club record for the highest number of league goals scored in a single season. Did they score 83, 103 or 123?

SEASON 2003-2004 - 1

21. What 'Wanderers' did United beat 4-0 at Old Trafford on the opening day of the season?

22. Can you name any 2 of United's 3 Group opponents in the UEFA Champions League?

23. What was the score of the game when United met Arsenal at Old Trafford in September?

24. Who scored his first Premier League goal for United against Blackburn Rovers in November at Old Trafford?

25. Name the club United beat in the FA Cup Semi-Final.

26. What South Coast club was the first team to beat United in the Premiership?

27. Who scored United's winner in the FA Cup Semi-Final?

28. What team put United out of the UEFA Champions League?

29. Name the team that unexpectedly beat United in the Premiership in January.

30. United suffered two consecutive 1-0 defeats towards the end of the season. Name either 1 of the 2 victorious teams.

LEGEND - OLE GUNNAR SOLSKJAER

31. How much did United pay for Ole Gunnar Solskjaer - £1 million, £1.5 million or £2 million?

32. Where in Norway was Ole born - Kristiansund, Sandefjord or Oslo?

33. Name either of his two previous clubs.

34. True or False, Ole scored on his United League debut?

35. Eric Cantona likened Ole to a former French team mate of his. What is the name of the player that Eric was referring to?

36. How many FA Carling Premier League goals did Ole score during the 1996-1997 season?

37. Ole scored on his Old Trafford European debut for the Reds. Can you recall United's Austrian opponents?

38. Against which North East club did Ole score his last goal of the 1996-1997 season for United?

39. True or False, Ole scored on his FA Cup debut for the Reds?

40. Ole scored twice for United in a 2-2 draw in a Premier League game on 3 May 1997. What City provided the opposition that day?

UNITED MANAGERS

41.   Who was in charge of United when they won the FA Cup in 1909?

42.   True or False, Frank O'Farrell was United's manager when the club were relegated to the Second Division at the end of the 1973-1974 season?

43.   In what year did Dave Sexton become the manager of Manchester United?

44.   What was the first major trophy that United won under the management of Alex Ferguson and in what year was it won?

45.   In what season did the Reds first win the First Division Championship under Matt Busby?

46.   How many Cup Finals did United appear in under the reign of Ron Atkinson?

47.   What was the highest league position that the Reds finished in under the management of Herbert Bamlett, United's manager between 1926-1932?

48.   How many times did United finish the season as Division 1 Runners-Up when Dave Sexton was manager?

49.   Which Manager, as opposed to the position of Club Secretary, did Matt Busby succeed at Old Trafford?

50.   Who was appointed United's manager when Sir Matt Busby retired at the end of the 1968-1969 season?

TRIVIA - 1

51. For whose Testimonial did United play Scunthorpe United on 17 December 1984?

52. United played a Fund raising match on 2 August 1982 away to Aldershot. For which Fund were they raising monies?

53. In what year did Newton Heath become Manchester United 1900, 1901 or 1902?

54. Which of the following names were suggested, before Manchester United was selected, to replace Newton Heath as the name of the club, Manchester Central, Manchester Royals or Manchester Town?

55. Old Trafford had a new Cantelever Stand built for the 1966 World Cup Finals. How much did it cost - £150,000, £350,000 or £550,000?

56. What name was given to United's first ever Youth Team?

57. What was significant about the Reds' 5-0 home win over Tottenham Hotspur at their Bank Street Ground in Clayton on 22 January 1910?

58. Can you name the legendary United player who was given a free transfer at the end of the 1920-1921 season?

59. United lost 5-0 to Everton at Goodison Park on 8 October 1927. Name the prolific Everton centre forward who scored all 5 goals?

60. How many goals did United concede during the 1930-1931 season 105, 110 or 115?

NEWTON HEATH - 1

61.   In what year was Newton Heath formed?

62.   The workers of which Railway Company's Carriage & Wagon Works formed Newton Heath?

63.   Why was Newton Heath's first ever FA Cup game awarded to their opponents despite the fact that the full time score was 2-2?

64.   In what season did Newton Heath first participate in The Football Combination - 1879-80, 1882-83 or 1888-89?

65.   In between the periods when the club played in The Football Combination and The Football League, what other structured league did they play in?

66.   By what nickname were Newton Heath known?

67.   What was the first Cup won by Newton Heath - the FA Cup, the Manchester Senior Cup or the Lancashire Cup?

68.   Where in Newton Heath did the club first play their home games?

69.   What was Newton Heath's highest ever finish in Division 1 - 2nd, 7th or 16th?

70.   In 1896 the club changed their colours. What colours (jerseys & shorts) did they originally play in and what colours replaced these?

GUESS MY NAME

71.   I joined United in November 1962 from non-league Maidstone United. Initially a centre-forward I was converted into a central defender and won a Championship medal in 1967 and a European Cup winners' medal in 1968.

72.   I made my United debut in an FA Cup tie against Sheffield Wednesday in 1958 and scored twice. I won two Championship medals and a European Cup winners' medal with the Reds during the 1960's.

73.   I signed for United in 1949. I made 683 appearances for the club and won Championship medals in 1956, 1957, 1965 & 1967. I was also the oldest member of United's European Cup winning side.

74.   I captained United to FA Cup glory in 1948 and won international caps for both the Republic of Ireland and Northern Ireland. In 1949 I was honoured with the Footballer of the Year Award.

75.   I was a Busby Babe and made my debut for the club in 1960. In 392 appearances for United I scored 28 times. In 1966 I won a World Cup winners' medal.

76.   I was born in Halesowen in 1971 and joined United in 1988. I won many honours at Old Trafford, before leaving in 1996, including a League Cup winners' medal in 1992 and 3 Championship medals (1993, 1994, 1996).

77.   I was born in West Ham, London and during the early part of my career I played for Fulham. Peter Schmeichel and I made our United league debuts on the opening day of the 1991-1992

season.

78.   I was born in Bury in 1975 and joined United as a trainee in 1991. I made my league debut for the club in the final game of the 1993-1994 season and won my first England cap in June 1995.

79.   I joined the Reds from Burnley in 1964 and in my first season at the club, I won a Championship medal. I was a member of England's 1966 World Cup winning squad and left Old Trafford in September 1966.

80.   I survived the Munich Air Disaster and was voted the Best Goalkeeper at the 1958 World Cup Finals. Although I was at Old Trafford from 1957-1966, I never won any honours with the club.

THE 1980's - 1

81.   On the day that Bryan Robson joined United, the Reds beat a Midlands club 5-0 at Old Trafford. Who scored a hat-trick in that game?

82.   How many London area clubs did United meet in their successful 1982-1983 FA Cup campaign?

83.   In what position did the Reds finish in Division 1 at the end of the 1985-1986 season?

84.   During the 1980's the Reds signed their first £1million player. Can you recall the season this took place?

85.   Who was paraded as the new owner of Manchester United when he juggled a football on the Old Trafford pitch on the opening day of the 1989-1990 season?

86.   Which London club did the Reds defeat in the Semi-Final of the 1983 Milk Cup?

87.   Can you recall the player who scored a penalty for the Reds in their 2-2 draw with Dundee United in the 1982-1983 UEFA Cup?

88.   During the 1984-1985 season, who played the most league games for the club Arthur Albiston, Gary Bailey or Bryan Robson?

89.   In what season was the system of 3 points for a win first introduced?

90.   United won their opening 10 games of the 1985-1986 season but can you recall the club which brought their winning run to an end?

CHAMPIONS 2006-07 – 1

91.   Against what London club did Ole Gunnar Solskjaer score his comeback goal?

92.   Who scored United's winner in their 1-0 win over Liverpool at Anfield?

93.   Can you recall the name of the famous manager of the European XI team that visited Old Trafford to face United in a Charity Match?

94.   What landmark appearance did Paul Scholes make in United's home game against Liverpool?

95.   United thumped this team 5-1 on the opening day of the season at Old Trafford. Name the London club.

96.   He scored the vitally important goal that gave United a 1-0 victory over Manchester City at Eastlands. Name him.

97.   How many points did United win the Premiership title with – 87, 88 or 89?

98.   Manchester United beat these new boys 2-0 at Old Trafford in their last game of 2006. Can you name the Premiership debutants?

99.   This player made his Premier League debut for United in their 3-1 win over Aston Villa at Old Trafford. Name him.

100.   What United player in season 2007-08 was the last player to score at Old Trafford in the Premiership during season 2006-07?

NAME THE TEAM - 1

*All you have to do here is name the players who played in the following
game. Players are numbered 1 - 11 for reference only.
(Please ignore the number of spaces between the players' names)*

The 1977 FA Cup Winning Team

1.   A--------S-------

2.   J-------N--------

3.   A-------A-----

4.   S-------M--------

5.   B------G--------

6.   M--------B-------

7.   S-------C------

8.   J-------G--------

9.   S--------P------

10.   L-------M------

11.   G------H------

Sub   D-------M-------

HISTORY - 1

101. How many times during the 1980's did United's Youth Team reach the Final of the FA Youth Cup?

102. Who scored the Reds' goal in their 1993 FA Charity Shield game against Arsenal at Wembley?

103. For what reason was Matt Busby in London on 9 July 1968?

104. How many FA Charity Shields did United contest during the 1950's?

105. What colour of shirts did United wear in the 1983 FA Charity Shield?

106. Which Children's Charity did the Reds donate autographed footballs to for their 1983 Appeal?

107. Name the United star who was voted European Footballer of the Year in 1964?

108. Can you name the Reds' player who was voted Irish Player of the Year in 1976.

109. How many FA Cup Finals, excluding Replays, did Gary Bailey appear in for United?

110. In season 1971-72 Old Trafford was the most expensive League Match Ticket Book priced at £15, £20 or £40?

LEGEND - BRYAN ROBSON

111.   Name the manager that brought Bryan to Old Trafford.

112.   To the nearest £250,000 how much did Bryan cost United?

113.   What was the first trophy Bryan won with United?

114.   What was Bryan's last season with United?

115.   What was Bryan's nickname at United?

116.   Name the club Bryan joined when he left Old Trafford.

117.   Whose help did he secure in December 2000 to help him at the club in Q116?

118.   How many England caps did he win 80, 90 or 100?

119.   What City was he appointed manager of in 2003?

120.   Who did Bryan replace at the Hawthorns in November 2004 as manger of West Bromwich Albion?

FA CUP - 1

121. Can you name the United striker who was sent off in the Reds' 3rd Round tie at Sheffield United on 9 January 1994?

122. Which member of the Royal Family handed Bryan Robson the FA Cup after United's 4-0 win over Brighton & Hove Albion in the 1983 Replay?

123. In the 4th Round of the 1989-1990 competition United visited Edgar Street. Name the United they played.

124. Name United's opponents at St James' Park for their 3rd Round game on 4 January 1969.

125. Name the Yorkshire side which the Reds defeated 4-0 in the 5th Round during season 1963-1964.

126. How many FA Cup winners' medals did Steve Coppell win during his Old Trafford career?

127. Who scored for United in the 1983 & 1985 Finals?

128. Name two of the three United players who were suspended for the Semi-Final with Oldham Athletic on 10 April 1994.

129. Which former United hero managed Peterborough United when they met the Reds in the 4th Round at Old Trafford on 24 January 1976?

130. Can you name the World Cup winner who scored against United for Spurs in a 3rd Round Replay at Old Trafford on 9 January 1980?

UNITED INTERNATIONALS - 1

131. Can you name the United defender who won his only Scotland cap against Denmark in 1975?

132. In which Scandinavian country did Denis Law hit a hat-trick in June 1963?

133. What was coincedental about Clayton Blackmore's first 3 appearances for Wales?

134. When Peter Schmeichel won a European Championship winners' medal with Denmark in 1992 he made a crucial save in the Semi-Final penalty shoot-out. Can you name the Dutch striker whose spot-kick he saved?

135. What did Bryan Robson break in the opening game of the 1987-1988 season?

136. How many World Cup Finals did George Best appear in?

137. A former United and Aberdeen player was awarded the OBE in the 1993 New Years Honours List. Name him.

138. Against which African team did Denis Law play his first game for Scotland in the World Cup Final stages?

139. In what competition did Ryan Giggs make his European debut for the Reds?

140. True or False, Norman Whiteside made his Northern Ireland debut in the Final stages of the World Cup?

SEASON 2002-2003 - 1

141. Who did United beat 1-0 at Old Trafford on the opening day of the season?

142. Who scored the winning goal in Q141?

143. Can you name the first team to beat United in the league this season?

144. Who scored both United goals in a 2-1 away win at Liverpool?

145. Against what team did Ruud score a hat-trick in a 5-3 win at Old Trafford in November?

146. Can you recall the side United beat 2-1 on New Years Day?

147. At what club's ground did United lift the Premier League trophy on the last day of the season?

148. To the nearest 5, how many points did United end the season with?

149. What was the score when Real Madrid visited Old Trafford in March?

150. Can you name the Swiss club that United played in the Group Stages of the UEFA Champions League?

TRIVIA - 2

151.   What was significant about Chas Richards goal for Manchester United against Gainsborough Town on 6 September 1902?

152.   How many of United's 4 goals did Ole Gunnar Solskjaer score against Newcastle United in the 1996 FA Charity Shield?

153.   In what season was Manchester United formed into a Limited Company 1906-07, 1946-47 or 1976-77?

154.   What was significant about the Reds' 1-0 victory over Stoke City in a First Division game on 3 September 1983?

155.   True or False, both Arthur Albiston and Steve Coppell played in all 42 of United's league games during the 1980-81 season?

156.   In what year during the 1980's did Sir Matt Busby become the Club President?

157.   Was United's average crowd 48,388 50,388 or 52,388 during their 1974-75 Second Division Championship winning season?

158.   Can you name the only United player to have played in both the 1985 and 1995 FA Cup Finals?

159.   True or False, Neil Webb played for United in an FA Premier League game?

160.   Who was the Reds' regular penalty taker during the 1990-1991 season?

THE 1960's

161. Which Lancashire team did United beat 3-1 in the 4th Round of the FA Cup on 30 April 1960?

162. Did Alex Stepney or David Gaskell make the most league appearances for the Reds during the 1966-67 season?

163. United lost their 1964 FA Cup Semi-Final to the eventual Cup winners that year. Name the London side they lost to.

164. George Best was the Reds' leading goalscorer in the league for season 1968-69. How many goals did he score 26, 28 or 30?

165. In what year did Denis Law join United?

166. Can you name the United player who missed the Reds' FA Cup 4th Round game at Old Trafford against Norwich City on 18 February 1967, thereby ending his run of 61 consecutive FA Cup games for the club?

167. In what position did United finish in Division 1 at the end of season 1960-61, 2nd, 7th or 19th?

168. United won the FA Cup in 1963, but can you recall the South Coast club which they defeated in the Semi-Final?

169. Both of United's full-backs played all 42 league games for the club during their 1964-65 Championship winning season. Name them.

170. Which team did United meet in the European Cup in both the 1965-66 and 1967-68 competitions?

SEASON 1997-1998 - 1

171. Who were the first team to beat United in a league game?

172. Against which team was Gary Pallister sent off in September 1997 only for his red card to be later quashed by the FA on appeal?

173. Who were the first Premiership side to score against the Reds?

174. True or False, United won their first 3 Premier League games of the season?

175. United beat Barnsley 7-0 at Old Trafford on 25 October 1997 and Andy Cole scored a hat-trick. Who scored the other 4 goals for the Reds?

176. In November 1997 United played 3 consecutive away games. Name any 2 of the 3 teams they played.

177. Who scored United's first goal of their Premier League campaign and who provided the opposition?

178. Name the Spurs defender who scored an own-goal in the game in Q177.

179. Can you name the United substitute who scored in the 2-2 draw with Chelsea at Old Trafford in September 1997?

180. Who scored United's winner against Southampton at Old Trafford on 13 August 1997?

LEGEND - ANDY COLE

181. Against what team did Andy Cole score his first hat-trick for United?

182. When United beat Liverpool at Anfield on 6 December 1997, how many times did Andy score?

183. In the game in Q182 whose slip let Andy in to score the opening goal of the game?

184. What shirt number did Andy wear in his first season at the club?

185. True or False, Andy was capped by England Schoolboys?

186. Andy broke his leg in a tackle with a Liverpool player during a reserve team game at the start of the 1996-97 season. Who did he tangle with?

187. In what year did he make his league debut for Arsenal?

188. How many of United's 4 goals did Andy score in their 4-0 European Cup Quarter-Final win over FC Porto in March 1997?

189. Against what City did he score his first Premier League goal during season 1997-98?

190. In what month and year did he sign for United?

LEGENDS - 1

191. How many major Cup medals did Nobby Stiles win with United's first team?

192. Can you name either of the two United stars that Wilf McGuinness dropped for the Reds' match against Everton at Goodison Park on 10 March 1969?

193. How many goals did Viv Anderson score for the Reds during his Old Trafford career 3, 4 or 5?

194. How many full England caps did Bill Foulkes win?

195. Bobby Charlton, Brian Kidd and Nobby Stiles have all managed the same club. Name the club concerned.

196. Which United player made all 42 league appearances for the club during the 1955-56 season?

197. After leaving Old Trafford Frank Stapleton played for Ajax Amsterdam and which French League side?

198. Which former Old Trafford hero did Glasgow Celtic Chairman, Fergus McCann, sack in June 1994?

199. Can you name the United manager who signed Ian Storey Moore?

200. Against which United player were Liverpool fans chanting Everton reject during a league game at Anfield on 31 March 1985?

NAME THE TEAM - 2

The 1964-65 First Division Championship Winning Team

1.   P--------D-----------

2.   S--------B---------

3.   T--------D-------

4.   B-------F----------

5.   P-------C--------

6.   N------S--------

7.   J-------C--------

8.   D------H------

9.   B--------C--------

10.   D--------L-----

11.   G-------B--------

TRIVIA - 3

201.   What stringed instrument did Mark Hughes play in his school orchestra?

202.   How many World Cup Finals (the Final Stages) did Bryan Robson play in?

203.   Was Sammy McIlroy awarded the CBE, MBE or OBE for his services to football?

204.   Which United player was voted Footballer of the Year by his peers in 1966?

205.   True or False, Sammy McIlroy played for Manchester City?

206.   Which former Liverpool manager advised Ron Atkinson to pay West Bromwich Albion whatever they wanted for Bryan Robson?

207.   In the 1983 PFA Award poll, which United player finished in second place just behind Liverpool's Kenny Dalglish?

208.   Who was ex-United player, Andy Ritchie, playing for when he visited Old Trafford on 19 March 1983?

209.   Name the United Assistant Manager who retired from Old Trafford in October 1971.

210.   How many times did Ron Atkinson win the Manager of the Year Award whilst he was in charge of United?

LEGEND - PAUL INCE

211. Where in London was Paul born?

212. From what club did United purchase Paul?

213. In what year did Paul arrive at Old Trafford?

214. What was the first trophy that Paul won with United?

215. What nickname did Paul (and many of the United fans) give himself during his time at United?

216. Name the club Paul joined when he left Old Trafford.

217. After 2 years in Italy, Paul returned to English football. What team did he sign for?

218. Against what club did Paul make his league debut for United - Millwall, Watford or Wimbledon?

219. Name the club Paul signed for in the summer of 2002.

220. Paul has played under the management of a former team mate. Name the player and the team concerned.

NAME MY FORMER CLUB

All you have to do here is match the player with the club he left to join Manchester United.

221.	Joe Jordan	Manchester City
222.	Gary Pallister	Cambridge United
223.	Colin Gibson	St James' Gate
224.	Ian Ure	Bournemouth
225.	Dion Dublin	Leeds United
226.	John Connelly	West Bromwich Albion
227.	Johnny Carey	Middlesbrough
228.	Sandy Turnbull	Aston Villa
229.	Ted MacDougall	Arsenal
230.	Maurice Setters	Burnley

LEGEND - DENIS LAW

231.   From what club did United sign Denis?

232.   In what year did Denis sign for United?

233.   To the nearest £15,000 how much did United pay for Denis?

234.   What was the first trophy Denis won with United?

235.   How many goals did Denis score for Man City in an FA Cup tie against Luton Town only for the game to be abandoned?

236.   At what Town did Denis begin his professional career?

237.   Can you name his Scottish team mate in Italy?

238.   What Football Award did Denis win in 1964?

239.   Denis played for 4 different managers at Old Trafford. Name any 3 of the 4.

240.   Against what Country did Denis make his international debut for Scotland - England, Northern Ireland or Wales?

THE LEAGUE CUP

241.   Who received the Man of the Match Award in the 1983 Final?

242.   Which one of the two Bristol teams, City or Rovers, did United play in the 3rd Round of the competition in 1973?

243.   In what Division of the Football League were Oxford United when United played them in the Cup in September 1973?

244.   Name the seaside club that eliminated the Reds from the Cup in season 1966-1967.

245.   In the 1994 Coca-Cola Cup Final, 3 of the players in the Final had played for both United and Aston Villa. Name them.

246.   How many United players have been sent off at Wembley in a League Cup Final?

247.   Who was in goal for the Reds when Manchester City beat them 4-0 in Round 4 of the 1975-76 Cup?

248.   Who did the Reds beat in the 1994 Semi-Final?

249.   Name the United defender who was sent off against Stockport County in a Round 2 game on 30 August 1978.

250.   True or False, Eric Cantona was suspended for the 1994 Final?

TRIVIA - 4

251. Can you name the Lancashire side that played Liverpool in the FA Cup Semi-Final at Old Trafford in 1971?

252. Who captained the Reds in the FA Cup Final of 1957?

253. Against which South American country did Bobby Charlton score his last goal for England - Brazil, Colombia or Uruguay?

254. Can you name the former United Northern Ireland International who wrote the book entitled 'Wild About Football'?

255. How many home European ties did United play at Maine Road 1, 2 or 3?

256. Name the United star of the 1950's & 1960's who was nicknamed Cowboy.

257. In what year did Newton Heath turn professional - 1880, 1885 or 1890?

258. Two United players played in all 42 league games during the 1966-1967 Championship winning season. Name either of them.

259. Which Midlands club did the Reds' Youth Team defeat in consecutive FA Youth Cup Finals during the 1950's?

260. How many FA Cup Finals did George Best appear in for the club?

ALMOST A RED

261. When Ron Atkinson became the United manager in 1981, which Tottenham Hotspur player did he attempt to sign?

262. Can you name the Queens Park Rangers star that Dave Sexton withdrew his interest in signing because of the player's injury problems?

263. Name the Arsenal defender of the 1970's & 1980's who was rejected by United after a trial at Old Trafford.

264. Which Queens Park Rangers goalkeeper did Dave Sexton attempt to sign in the late 1970's before the player decided to join West Ham United?

265. Name the Chilean striker who rejected a move to Old Trafford in December 1997?

266. For which Argentinean club did the above Chilean striker play for at the time?

267. Name the Glasgow Celtic forward who Ron Atkinson attempted to sign during the early 1980's.

268. A number of times during 1997, Alex Ferguson attempted to lure a Barcelona defender to United. Name the player concerned.

269. In season 1978-1979 Dave Sexton attempted to sign Coventry City's goalkeeper. Did he try to sign Steve Ogrizovic or Jim Blyth?

270. Ron Atkinson attempted to sign a Brighton & Hove Albion defender in 1981. Name the future Liverpool star.

EUROPEAN CUP WINNERS' CUP

271. United played their first ever ECWC game in a stadium where they won a European trophy. Can you name the stadium?

272. Can you name the United player who was brought down by Legia Warsaw's Jozwiak, during the 1990-1991 competition, and which resulted in the Legia player being sent off?

273. Who managed Barcelona when United beat them in their Quarter-Final tie in 1984?

274. What Greek side were the first side United met in the competition after winning it in 1991?

275. How far did United progress in the 1977-1978 competition - Round 2, Quarter-Final or Semi-Final?

276. When United met Wrexham in the 1990-1991 ECWC, which Division of the Football League did the Welsh side play in?

277. Name the Welsh winger who scored for United in their 1-1 draw with Juventus in the Semi-Final, 1st leg at Old Trafford in 1984.

278. Name the English side who became the first team to beat United in a ECWC game.

279. Who scored for United in their 1-1 draw with Atletico Madrid in Round 2 of the 1991-1992 competition.

280. In the 1990-1991 ECWC Barcelona's Spanish international goalkeeper was suspended for the Final. Name him.

NANI

281. How much did Manchester United pay for the services of Nani - £17m, £18m or £19m?

282. From what club did United sign Nani?

283. What is Nani's full name?

284. In which Portuguese colony off the coast of Africa was Nani born?

285. Against what club did he score his first Premier League goal for Manchester United?

286. What team does Nani support?

287. Can you recall the name of the Russian team he scored a magnificent solo goal against in the 2005-06 Uefa Champions League?

288. Nani made his international debut for Portugal against a team from Scandinavia. Name them.

289. What shirt number does he wear for Portugal?

290. How old was Nani when he signed for Manchester United?

HISTORY - 2

291. Can you name the Award that Ron Atkinson won for the first time in February 1983?

292. Who was Coventry City's manager when United met them at Highfield Road on 29 August 1981?

293. Who appropriately scored the Reds' 100th goal of the 1993-1994 season?

294. In what position did United star, Harry Moger, play for the club between 1903 - 1912?

295. Name the defender who missed a penalty in the FA Charity Shield penalty shoot-out in August 1993.

296. Three players with the first name Alex have played for United since the end of the Second World War. Name any two of them.

297. What Award did Bryan Robson receive in December 1989?

298. Can you recall the manufacturer of United's 1979 FA Cup Final kit?

299. True or False, United were the first club to concede a goal in the FA Carling Premier League?

300. The father of a post-war Manchester United manager fought for the Great Britain Middleweight Boxing Title in 1933. Name the manager.

NAME THE TEAM - 3

The 1992 Rumbelows League Cup Winning Team

1.   P--------S---------

2.   P-------P-------

3.   D--------I------

4.   S-------B--------

5.   M-------P--------

6.   G------P--------

7.   A------K--------

8.   P------I--------

9.   B--------M-------

10.   M-------H----------

11.   R------G------

LEGEND - STEVE BRUCE

301. What injury did Steve sustain when he made his league debut for the Reds?

302. At which Football League club did he begin his professional career?

303. Why did Steve miss United's 1996 FA Cup Final success over Liverpool?

304. Steve directed a video in 1993 about Manchester United. What was it called?

305. In what year did he join United?

306. Against which Yorkshire side did he miss a penalty in an FA Cup 5th Round game in February 1993?

307. Where was Steve born - Gillingham, Newcastle or Norwich?

308. Against which London club did he score his first league goal of United's 1993-1994 Double winning season?

309. United drew 3-3 with Liverpool at Anfield on 4 January 1994. Did Steve score the Reds' first, second or third goal?

310. When Steve was at Old Trafford both he and his defensive partner, Gary Pallister, were given nicknames. What were the pair known as?

THE 1970's

311. During season 1977-1978 the Reds were twice beaten at Old Trafford by clubs from the Midlands. Name either of them.

312. Which Italian Serie A team did United play at Old Trafford on 20 October 1976?

313. True or False, United were the first club to display advertising on their shirts in 1979?

314. What Scottish club did George Best join after he left Fulham?

315. What was the title of the record on sale at the Manchester United souvenir shop to commemorate United's return to Division 1 in season 1975-1976?

316. Two United players were nominated for the 1976 Young Player of the Year Award. Name either of them.

317. When Jim Holton left Old Trafford in December 1974, which North-East club did he join?

318. What happened at Old Trafford on 4 July 1977?

319. Can you recall the name of the Arsenal player who scored the winning goal against United in the 1979 FA Cup Final?

320. In season 1975-76, United's matchday programme (United Review) included advertisements to deter something. What were the advertisements trying to deter?

LEGEND - BOBBY CHARLTON

321. In what year did Bobby win his first FA Youth Cup Winners' medal with United - 1952, 1953 or 1954?

322. Ironically, what team did Bobby Charlton make his league debut for United against?

323. What was the first trophy Bobby won with United as a Professional player?

324. Bobby holds the record for the most appearances for United. What player lies in second place?

325. In what Tournament did Bobby play his last ever game for United on 2nd May 1973?

326. Against what team did he score his last league goal for United - Chelsea, Liverpool or Southampton?

327. In what year did he make his international debut for England?

328. Can you name Bobby's famous brother who played for Leeds United?

329. What 2 Football Awards did Bobby win in 1966?

330. To the nearest 25, how many goals in total did Bobby score for United?

SPONSORS & ADVERTISEMENTS

331. Which make of bra did George Best star in a commercial for in 1977?

332. Can you recall the model of Ford car which appeared on the back page of the United Review in 1973?

333. Which sportswear company manufactures David Beckham's football boots?

334. Which company became the official sponsors of Manchester United during the 1978-1979 season?

335. What colour of Hummel football boots did United's Ian Storey-Moore wear during the early 1970's?

336. Can you name the Greeting Card business which first owned the marketing rights to United's mascot, Fred The Red?

337. Name the Irish player who modelled the MUFC Winter Jacket in the matchday programmes during the 1982-1983 season.

338. What is the name of the sportswear company that made United's FA Cup Final shirts for both the 1983 & 1985 Finals?

339. During the 1997-1998 season both Gary & Phil Neville were sponsored by the same sportswear manufacturer. Name the company concerned.

340. Name the brewery who sponsored the 6-a-side tournament which United entered in 1986.

FIND THE PLAYER

*ALL YOU HAVE TO DO HERE IS UNSCRAMBLE THE LETTERS
TO FIND THE PLAYER'S NAME*

341.	LSSREUL	DREEBMOASR	7, 10
342.	KIME	LHPANE	4, 6
343.	YDNAN	LLECAAW	5, 7
344.	RYARH	RGGEG	5, 5
345.	HOJN	NOCLENLY	4, 8
346.	RENARW	BDELYAR	6, 7
347.	LEON	WLANLCET	4, 8
348.	GORER	NBERY	5, 5
349.	OACLR	RATSOI	5,6
350.	VDAID	KALSELG	5, 7

TRIVIA - 5

351. How many players did Alex Ferguson sell to Manchester United when he was in charge of Aberdeen?

352. At the last home game of the 1996-1997 season, 5 players took to the Old Trafford pitch with Championship trophies. Four of the five were United captains displaying their respective league titles. Who was the fifth player?

353. Who was United's Youth Team Coach during the 1996-1997 season?

354. When Phil Neville made his full International debut for England, did he become the first, second or third youngest player to represent England?

355. In 1997 a video cassette was released in which Alex Ferguson had to select his best ever United side. What was the title of the video?

356. Name the former United goalkeeper who is the Chairman of the South African Manchester United Supporters Club.

357. Was Mick Martin (Midfielder 1972-1975) born in Cork, Dublin or Galway?

358. How many FA Cup Finals did Jimmy Nicholl appear in for United?

359. In what year did United last win the First Division Championship?

360. United released a compact disc single just before Christmas 1997. What was it called?

FA CUP FINALS

361. What colour of shirts did United wear in the 1948 Final?

362. How many FA Cup Finals did the Reds appear in during the 1950's?

363. When United met Liverpool in the 1977 Final, did a standing ticket for the game cost £2.50, £5.50 or £7.50?

364. Why was Kevin Moran not handed a winners' medal when he passed the Royal Box after the 1985 Final?

365. Whose place in the United side did Arthur Albiston take for the 1977 Final?

366. Name the four Irishmen who played for the Reds in the 1985 Final.

367. How many FA Cup Finals did Denis Law appear in during his career with Huddersfield Town, Manchester City and United?

368. Name the United player who won the Man of the Match Award in the 1977 Final.

369. Can you name the United forward who scored 2 goals in the 1948 Final?

370. Name the former United player who set up the winning goal in the 1976 FA Cup Final.

AN EARLY BATH

All you have to do here is match the player with the game in which he was sent off.

371. Mark Hughes   1994 v Aston Villa (League Cup Final)

372. Eric Cantona   1995 v York City (League Cup)

373. Roy Keane   1993 v Galatasaray (European Cup)

374. Nicky Butt   1992 v Moscow Torpedo (UEFA Cup)

375. Eric Cantona   1995 v Middlesbrough (Premier League)

376. Pat McGibbon   1994 v Glasgow Rangers (Friendly)

377. Peter Schmeichel   1995 v Blackburn R. (Premier League)

378. Andrei Kanchelskis   1994 v Arsenal (Premier League)

379. Eric Cantona   1996 v West Ham Utd (Premier League)

380. Roy Keane   1994 v Charlton Athletic (FA Cup)

SPOT THE PLAYER

All you have to do here is pick out the 10 players who have played for United. There is one player on each line.

381. William Wrigglesworth, James Arkwright, Cecil Carson

382. Mick Devlin, Jeff Whitefoot, David Jones

383. Samuel Blacksmith, Henry Cockburn, Harry Appleton

384. Ian Silcock, Frank Blunstone, Wilson Greenwood

385. Frank Bristol, Horace Blew, John Beadsworth

386. Alan Foggon, Jeffrey Irons, Wallace Peddie

387. Arnold Sidebottom, Colin Sarvis, Peter Rogers

388. Peter Quinn, Stanley Gallimore, Frank Muller

389. Edward Gaston, Neil Denton, Albert Quixall

390. John Moody, Frank Tittle, John White

CHARITY SHIELD

391. In the 1997 FA Charity Shield Peter Schmeichel saved a penalty from a Chelsea player. Name the player.

392. Who scored the winning penalty for United in the game in Q391?

393. United played their first ever FA Charity Shield game in 1908. Which London side did they beat after a Replay?

394. Excluding Replays, how many FA Charity Shields have United played in 15, 17 or 21?

395. In what year did the Reds last share the Shield?

396. Between 1963 and 1990, United played in 7 FA Charity Shields. In six of the games the Reds played Merseyside opposition. Which London club made up the seventh encounter?

397. True or False, United's record score in the FA Charity Shield is 8-4?

398. Who has scored the most goals for the Reds in FA Charity Shield, Bobby Charlton, Harold Halse or Billy Meredith?

399. In what year, prior to their 1998 defeat by Arsenal, did the Reds last lose an FA Charity Shield?

400. How many times have United met Liverpool in the FA Charity Shield?

NAME THE TEAM - 4

The 1983 FA Cup Winning Team

1.   G--------B--------

2.   M-------D-------

3.   A-------A------

4.   R-----W------

5.   K-----M--------

6.   G-------M--------

7.   B--------R-------

8.   A-------M-------

9.   F------S---------

10.   N--------W--------

11.   A--------D-------

THE CAPTAIN'S ARMBAND

From the clues given, you have to identify the Manchester United captain

401.   I was born in Aberdeen on 6 March 1949. I appeared in 3 FA Cup Finals for the Reds during the 1970's. When I left Old Trafford I joined Oldham Athletic.

402.   I also played for both Chelsea & Arsenal. Tommy Docherty made me his first signing in 1972. I later enjoyed a successful managerial career at a London club.

403.   I started my career at Burnley and joined United from Norwich City. I made 145 appearances for the Reds, scoring 3 goals.

404.   I was born in Glasgow on 19 February 1939 and made almost 400 appearances for the Reds. Three months after joining United from Glasgow Celtic, I won an FA Cup winners' medal.

405.   I won League Championship winners' medals with the Reds in 1956 & 1957. In the 1957 FA Cup Final I broke my cheekbone and was replaced in goal by a team mate.

406.   I joined United in 1979 and was with them until 1984. I won an FA Cup winners' medal in 1983, scoring in the Final.

407.   I was born on 11 January 1957. When I joined the Reds in 1981 I teamed up with my former manager at The Hawthorns.

408.   I played both football & cricket for the Republic of Ireland. In 1963 I led United to FA Cup glory over Leicester City.

409.   Alex Ferguson signed me in 1987 and I made over 400 appearances for the Reds. In 1996 I left Old Trafford for a club in the Midlands.

410.   I cost United £900,000 in August 1981. In 1983 I became the first player to score in two Wembley FA Cup Finals for two different clubs. I won a second FA Cup winners' medal with United in 1985.

LEGENDS - 2

411.   What team were Brian Kidd and Frank Stapleton playing
        when they visited Old Trafford on 18 October 1975?

412.   Can you name the United forward who was voted the Manchester
        United Player Of The Year for the 1978-1979 season?

413.   Who arrived at Old Trafford on loan from Real Madrid in March
        1983?

414.   Who scored the winner for the Reds in their Milk Cup Round 3
        win over West Ham United in 1985?

415.   Which former United goalkeeper won a European Cup Winners'
        medal in 1982?

416.   Where in England was Maurice Setters born?

417.   Two United players were selected to play for Wales in their
        World Cup Qualifying game against Iceland in 1984. Mark
        Hughes was one of them. Name the other.

418.   When John Aston Jnr. retired from football did he open a cafe, a
        pet shop or a sports shop?

419.   True or False, Duncan Edwards scored on his league debut for
        the Reds?

420.   When Terry Gibson and Ashley Grimes played against United at
        Old Trafford on 21 April 1984, which team were they playing
        for?

THE MANAGEMENT GAME

421. How much was the most money spent by Tommy Docherty on a player for Manchester United - £200,000 £375,000 or £450,000?

422. Name either of the two players who cost Tommy Docherty the fee in Q421.

423. Which Lancashire club beginning with the letter R did Jimmy Greenhoff manage in 1983?

424. When Dave Sexton left Old Trafford he became the manager of a Midlands club. Name them.

425. What London team was Dave Sexton in charge of when his side visited Old Trafford in August 1970?

426. Before becoming the manager of Middlesbrough, Bryan Robson had talks with a club from the Midlands about their vacant manager's job. Name the club concerned.

427. A future Manchester United manager won the Bells Manager Of The Year Award for Division 4 in the 1976-1977 season. Can you name him?

428. Two Manchester United managers have also managed the Scottish National Team since 1945. Name both of them.

429. Name the Midlands club that both Nobby Stiles & Stuart Pearson have been the Assistant Manager of.

430. Can you recall the United manager who allowed Denis Law to leave Old Trafford on a free transfer?

MIXED BAG - 1

431. Which one of the following seasons was Bryan Robson's most productive, in terms of goals scored - 1981-1982, 1982-1983 or 1983-1984?

432. Can you recall the BBC Sports Quiz Show which Ryan Giggs appeared on in March 1994?

433. Which Turkish team scored an own goal against United during the 1993-1994 season?

434. A brother of a famous United player had the name Busby as a middle name. Can you name the player concerned?

435. Who did Alex Ferguson replace as the manager of Aberdeen?

436. United played Red Star Belgrade in a friendly game in 1951. Which Festival was the game played to commemorate?

437. When Peter Bodak and John Gidman left Old Trafford they both joined the same club. What City did they join?

438. The Manchester United Team made a tv appearance in 1994 on a show hosted by Cilla Black. Name the show.

439. In season 1963-1964 did United finish in 2nd, 11th or 18th position in Division 1?

440. Can you name the London jail, beginning with the letter P, where George Best spent 8 days after a drink-driving offence during the 1980s?

ENGLAND UNITED

441. England's full-backs against Northern Ireland in October 1954 were both United players. Name either of them.

442. Name the Reds' star who signed a new 7 year contract with the club in October 1984.

443. Can you name the United midfielder who scored a penalty for the Reds in their 1-1 draw with Dukla Prague in the 1983-1984 European Cup Winners' Cup?

444. In what year was Gary Bailey capped by England for the first time?

445. Which Yorkshire side did Brian Greenhoff sign for when he left Old Trafford?

446. Name the United star of the 1980s & 1990s who was the patron of a Scanner Appeal which was named after him.

447. Who was United's No.8 in the 1990 FA Cup Final draw with Crystal Palace?

448. Can you name the United forward who made his international debut for England against Wales in 1976?

449. True or False, John Gidman won his one and only England cap after he joined United?

450. In what year did Ray Wilkins win his first cap for England in - 1976, 1977 or 1978?

TRIVIA - 6

451. True or False, Mark Hughes was never on a losing side for United in an FA Cup tie when he scored in the game?

452. Against what London team did Denis Irwin make his comeback in Season 1997-1998, after being badly hurt in a UEFA Champions League game away to Feyenoord?

453. How many FA Charity Shields did United play in during the 1970's?

454. United beat Everton at Goodison Park on 26 December 1977. What was the score of the game 6-0, 6-2 or 6-4?

455. Name the overseas player who scored twice for the Reds in their 5-0 home win over Leicester City on 13 September 1980.

456. Can you recall the United manager who brought Gary Bailey to Old Trafford?

457. United beat Anderlecht 10-0 in a European Cup tie on 26 September 1956. Name either of the two players who scored at least a hat-trick in the game.

458. How many of England's games did Alex Stepney play in during the 1970 World Cup Finals in Mexico?

459. Who was in goal for United in both legs of their 1969 European Cup Semi-Final clash with AC Milan?

460. In what year did Gordon Strachan sign for United?

MOVING ON - 1

All you have to do here is match the United player with the club he joined when he left Old Trafford.

461.	Andrei Kanchelskis	Dundee
462.	Gary Walsh	Chelsea
463.	Mike Phelan	Leicester City
464.	Colin McKee	Sheffield Wednesday
465.	Mark Robins	Middlesbrough
466.	Keith Gillespie	Everton
467.	Mal Donaghy	Kilmarnock
468.	Viv Anderson	West Bromwich Albion
469.	Jim Leighton	Norwich City
470.	Colin Gibson	Newcastle United

SEASON 1997-1998 - 2

471. What Lodnon club was the last team to defeat United in the Premier League?

472. United won an important away Premier League game on Monday 6 April 1998. Which Lancashire side did they defeat and what was the score of the game?

473. What United was the last to score against United in a Premier League game?

474. Can you name the French side which ended United's European Champions League dreams?

475. In 2 of the Reds' last 3 league games they won the game 3-0. Name either of the two sides which were on the receiving end?

476. Can you name the young Red who made his senior debut for the club against Leeds United at Old Trafford?

477. Who did United play in the final league game of the season?

478. What was the score of the game in Q477 and can you recall who scored for the Reds?

479. Name the young United player who made his debut for the club in the final game of the season.

480. How many points did United finish the season behind Arsenal?

NAME A TEAM

481. Name 2 foreign sides beginning with the letter A which United have played.

482. True or False, United have played a Copenhagen XI team?

483. Name the Czechoslovakian side beginning with the letter D which United have played in European competition.

484. Name the Hungarian team which beat United in the semi-final of the 1964-65 Inter Cities Fairs Cup.

485. Can you name the team from Belfast beginning with the letter G which United have played in a friendly?

486. Did United once play Hannover 1896, Hannover 1906 or Hannover 1946 in a friendly?

487. Name the Israeli team which United have played in a friendly?

488. True or False, Newtron Heath played a side named New Brighton Tower during the 1900-01 season?

489. Apart from Red Star Belgrade which other club from Belgrade have United played in the European Cup?

490. Name the two Spanish teams which United played in their very first European campaign during season 1956-57.

THE BOSS

491. Name the two European trophies Aberdeen won when Alex Ferguson managed them.

492. From which club did Glasgow Rangers sign the young Ferguson?

493. How much did Glasgow Rangers pay for his services - £55,000, £75,000 or £95,000?

494. What was so significant about the transfer fee in Q493?

495. Can you name the horse which gave Alex a winning start to his career as a racehorse owner?

496. Is the horse in Q495 named after a steam train, a Scottish town or a ship?

497. At which club was Alex once the Player-Manager?

498. How many times during his career as a professional footballer was he sent off?

499. How many games did Scotland win at the 1986 World Cup Finals when he was in charge of the national side?

500. How many Scottish League Cups did Aberdeen win under Alex?

NAME THE TEAM - 5

The 1968 European Cup Winning Team

1.   A--------S---------

2.   S------B---------

3.   T------D--------

4.   P------C-------

5.   B-----F-------

6.   N--------S------

7.   G---------B------

8.   B------K-----

9.   B------C----------

10.   D-------S----------

11.   J-------A--------

NAME THE YEAR - 1

501.   Ryan Wilson (Giggs) signs for United, Brian Kidd takes
        charge of United's Youth Policy and the Reds finish Division 1
        Runners-Up.

502.   United are floated on the Stock Exchange, Andrei Kanchelskis
        and Peter Schmeichel arrive at Old Trafford.

503.   George Best plays his final game for United and the Reds are
        relegated to Division 2.

504.   United manager, Dave Sexton, signs Joe Jordan and Gordon
        McQueen from Leeds United. The Reds lose to West Bromwich
        Albion in the FA Cup and are 10th in Division 1.

505.   United are Premier League Champions, Darren Ferguson joins
        Wolverhampton Wanderers and the Reds beat Wimbledon 3-0 in
        the 5th Round of the FA Cup at Selhurst Park.

506.   United are beaten in the World Club Championship, Denis Law
        scores 7 goals against Waterford in the European Cup and the
        Reds are Division 1 Runners-Up.

507.   United lose the FA Cup Final to Bolton Wanderers, Albert
        Quixall joins United from Sheffield Wednesday for a British
        record fee of £45,000.

508.   Granada's World In Action programme accuses United of corrupt
        and fraudulent practices, Joe Jordan is United's top goalscorer
        with 13 league goals and the Reds end the season as Division 1
        Runners-Up.

509.   United win the FA Cup, Paddy Crerand arrives from Glasgow
       Celtic and George Best makes his league debut versus West
       Bromwich Albion at Old Trafford.

510.   Dave Sexton is sacked and Ron Atkinson is appointed manager.
       Atkinson signs John Gidman, Frank Stapleton, Bryan Robson
       Remi Moses.

SEASON 1998-1999 - 1

511.   Against what Yorkshire Premier League side did Teddy Sheringham score the 250th senior goal of his career?

512.   How many Premier League goals did Dwight Yorke score during the season - 18, 19 or 20?

513.   Against what United did Andy Cole & Dwight Yorke score the 50th goal of their strike partnership on 25th April 1999?

514.   Name the former United goalkeeper who was part of Bradford City's successful promotion winning side during the 1998-1999 season.

515.   Who were the only team to prevent the Reds from scoring in the league at Old Trafford during the season?

516.   Against what Yorkshire team did David May taste his first Premiership action when he came on as a substitute in April?

517.   How may defeats did United suffer in the Premier League during the season?

518.   Name the United defender who came on as a substitute for Wes Brown in the Reds home game with Newcastle United and who was later substituted himself.

519.   What London club did the Reds beat 1-0 thanks to a very late Dwight Yorke goal in January?

520.   How many league goals did United score during the season - 80, 81 or 82?

CUP COMPETITIONS

521.   Name the Midlands club which put the Reds out of the 1972-1973 FA Cup.

522.   In the Final of which competition did a United team defeat Swindon Town during the 1963-1964 season?

523.   Can you recall the Irish club which United began the defence of the European Cup against during the 1968-1969 season?

524.   Can you name the Dutch side who were United's opponents in the UEFA Cup during the 1976-1977 season?

525.   This Spanish side became the first team to defeat United in 12 games in the European Cup Winners' Cup when the Reds lost a Round 2, 1st leg game on 23 October 1991. Name them.

526.   How many times did United reach the Semi-Final stage of the League Cup during the 1980's?

527.   At which club's ground did United beat Oldham Athletic 2-1, after extra-time, in the Semi-Final Replay of the 1989-90 FA Cup?

528.   How many games did United lose on their way to winning the European Cup in 1968?

529.   Which City put United, the holders of the FA Cup, out of the competition in 1990-91?

530.   Who scored United's winning goal, against Middlesbrough in extra-time, in the Semi-Final, 2nd leg of the 1991-92 League Cup?

ALL MIXED UP

531. Can you name the United player who made his debut for the club against Middlesbrough [a] on 22 October 1981 and who went on to make a total of 188 appearances for the Reds before injury forced him to retire?

532. In what season during the 1980's did United meet Raba Vasas ETO in the UEFA Cup?

533. True or False, Lou Macari played in Glasgow Celtic's 1971 League Cup Final loss to Partick Thistle?

534. Name the former United player who was appointed England manager in 1946.

535. Who became the first Manchester United player to score for England under Glenn Hoddle's reign as manager?

536. Name the Spanish League club Jordi Cruyff joined on loan during the 1998-1999 season.

537. When Manchester United purchased Dwight Yorke for £12.6 million, did he become the 5th, 6th or 7th most expensive footballer in the world?

538. In February 1999 a bronze statue was unveiled at the Old Trafford Museum. Who was the statue a tribute to?

539. Who did United sign on 5 February 1999?

540. Only one current United player played for Newcastle United against Glasgow Celtic in Peter Beardsley's Testimonial game on 27 January 1999. Name him.

LEGENDS - 3

541. True or False, George Best was sacked by Manchester United on the same day that the club sacked manager, Frank O' Farrell?

542. From which London club did United sign David Herd?

543. Name the West Bromwich Albion wing-half Matt Busby signed for £30,000 in January 1960.

544. Did United goalkeeper Ray Wood make 205, 305 or 405 appearances for the Reds?

545. When record signing John Downie joined United from Bradford Park Avenue in 1949 did he cost the club £8,000, £18,000 or £28,000?

546. Can you name the future Dutch manager of a Premier League club that Mark Hughes played for Barcelona against during the 1980's?

547. What club did Brian Kidd join after leaving Old Trafford in a £110,00 deal in 1974?

548. Who was the Reds' goalkeeper who was bundled into the net by Bolton Wanderers' Nat Lofthouse in the 1958 FA Cup Final?

549. Can you name the Lancashire club Albert Quixall joined when he left Old Trafford?

550. When United placed George Best on the transfer list in December 1972, can you recall to the nearest £50,000 how much they were asking for him?

UNITED IN PRINT

All you have to do here is re-arrange the player/manager to match him up with the book he wrote.

551.	George Best	United - We Shall Not Be Moved
552.	Noel Cantwell	Call The Doc
553.	Alex Stepney	For Club And Country
554.	Lou Macari	In Safe Keeping
555.	Denis Law	United We Stand
556.	Harry Gregg	Matt, United And Me
557.	Tommy Docherty	Wild About Football
558.	Alan Gowling	Living For Kicks
559.	Gary & Philip Neville	Best Of Both Worlds
560.	Jimmy Murphy	Football Inside Out

LEGEND - PADDY CRERAND

561.   At what club did Paddy begin his Professional career?

562.   In what year did Paddy sign for United?

563.   In what year did Paddy make his International debut for Scotland - 1960, 1961 or 1962?

564.   How many caps did Paddy win for Scotland - 16, 26 or 36?

565.   To the nearest 30, how many league appearances did Paddy make for United?

566.   Can you name the seaside club Paddy made his United debut against?

567.   Against what Yugoslavian club was Paddy sent off in the European Cup Semi-Final in 1966?

568.   What was the first trophy Paddy won at Old Trafford?

569.   Name the United manager that Paddy was an Assistant to at Old Trafford after he stopped playing.

570.   What Town did Paddy become the manager of in 1976?

1998-1999 PRE-SEASON

571. What Town did Ben Thornley join after leaving Old Trafford in the summer of 1998?

572. Sadly for all United fans a legendary striker died during the close season. Can you name him?

573. What goalkeeper became the first United player to leave the club on a free transfer under the Bosman ruling?

574. What Scottish club did Brian McClair join during the close season?

575. Who was voted United's Player of the Year for the 1997-98 season Gary Neville, Andy Cole or Ryan Giggs?

576. What goal did United fans vote as the best goal of the 1997-98 season - David Beckham's versus Liverpool, Ryan Giggs' versus Juventus or Andy Cole's versus Blackburn Rovers?

577. Can you name the Dutch striker who was linked with a move to the Reds after the World Cup?

578. What club did the player in Q577 eventually join?

579. During the close season United loaned Michael Twiss to a First Division club. Name the United he joined.

580. Which former Old Trafford hero was the manager of the team in Q579 at the time?

MUNICH MEMORIAL GAME

581. When Eric Cantona played in the above game how many days had it been since his last appearance at Old Trafford - 457, 477 or 497 days?

582. Who captained Manchester United on the night?

583. What was the official name of Eric's team?

584. What was the score at half-time?

585. Can you name the Swedish Blackburn Rovers striker who scored for United's opponents?

586. A young United player came on as a substitute and scored for Eric's team. Name the Mark concerned.

587. How many former United players played for the opposition?

588. Name the 1998 World Cup winning defender who scored against Manchester United.

589. The star of the night was undoubtedly the opposition's goalkeeper. Can you recall his name?

590. What was the final score of the game?

TRIVIA - 7

591.   Name the former United goalkeeper who left his coaching job in Kuwait and later took up a position on United's coaching staff in 1978.

592.   Can you name the Japanese midfield player who was reputedly linked to United in September 1998?

593.   What club was no. 592 with at the time?

594.   A member of the United team which finished Runners-Up in the Premiership during the 1997-1998 season played in the 1991 FA Charity Shield. Name him.

595.   What club was no. 594 playing for at the time and who were the opponents?

596.   Which First Division club made a £3million offer for Teddy Sheringham in September 1998?

597.   Can you name the former United player who David Beckham replaced as substitute in England's 1998 France World Cup game against Romania?

598.   In United's 1998-1999 UEFA Champions League Group the manager of Bayern Munich, Ottmar Hitzfeld, also managed a team which United met in the 1996-1997 competition. Name the team.

599.   Which club did Ole Gunnar Solskjaer refuse a move to a few weeks after the 1998-1999 season kicked off?

600.   How much was BskyB's first bid for Manchester United?

NAME THE TEAM - 6

The 1994 FA Cup Winning Team

1.   P------S-----------

2.   P------P----------

3.   D-------I---------

4.   S-------B--------

5.   A-------K---------

6.   G-----P----------

7.   E-----C----------

8.   P-----I-------

9.   R-------K-------

10.   M-------H-----------

11.   R-------G--------

SEASON 1999-2000 - 1

601. Name the United striker who scored in the 1-1 draw with Everton on the opening day of the season.

602. What Yorkshire club did United beat 4-0 at Old Trafford in August?

603. Name any team United played in the FA Cup during the season.

604. Can you name the United player who scored a hat-trick against his previous club in August in United's 5-1 victory?

605. How many of their 38 Premiership games did United win - 24, 26 or 28?

606. Name the team that beat United 5-0 in October.

607. What Italian Serie A side did United beat 3-1 at Old Trafford in the UEFA Champions League?

608. Can you recall the team United hammered 7-1 at Old Trafford on 1st April?

609. Can you recall the Dutch player who scored for United in a 3-2 away win at Watford in April?

610. A United player scored against a team he would later join in the Quarter-Finals of the UEFA Champions League. Name the player concerned.

HISTORY - 3

611. True or False, when United won the 1948 FA Cup they did not play any of their ties at Old Trafford.

612. What type of animal was United's mascot when they won the 1907-1908 First Division Championship?

613. Which Midlands club finished Runners-Up to United in the 1907-1908 Championship race?

614. Who played in goal for United in the 1958 FA Cup Final?

615. Who was United's captain for the 1958 FA Cup Final?

616. By what name were the United players who went on strike in the early 1900's known - The Ruffians, The Red Defenders or The Outcasts?

617. For what reason did the players in Q616 go on strike?

618. Can you name the United forward who scored a hat-trick in the Reds 3-1 FA Cup 3rd Round win over Workington Town in the 1957-1958 competition?

619. True or False, Manchester United's home jersey during season 1913-1914 was an all white shirt?

620. Who replaced Ernest Mangnall as manager of Manchester United - John Robson or John Chapman?

TRIVIA - 8

621. Against which club did Denis Law score 6 goals in an FA Cup tie for Manchester City only for the game to be abandoned?

622. True or False, Lou Macari & Frank Stapleton never played in the same Manchester United side.

623. Can you recall the Southampton midfielder who was reputedly linked with a move to United in October 1998?

624. On 31 January 1998 United lost their first Premiership game at Old Trafford in 10 months. What City beat them?

625. Can you recall the United defender who came on as a substitute in Q624 only to be substituted himself later in the game?

626. Which London club proved to be United's biggest attraction of the 1997-98 Premier League campaign with 55,306 fans in attendance?

627. In season 1998-99, against which European club did United score their first away goal of the season?

628. How many points did the Reds finish behind Arsenal in the 1997-98 Championship race?

629. How many of United's home Premier League games in season 1997-98 attracted a crowd of less than 55,000?

630. When United played Bayern Munich in the 1998-99 UEFA Champions League a former German World Cup winning captain played for the opposition. Name him.

SEASON 1998-1999 - 2

631. What City provided United's first league opposition of the season?

632. What was the score of the game in Q631?

633. Who scored the Reds' first Premier League goal of the season?

634. Against what London club did United record their first Premiership win of the season?

635. Who became the first club to defeat United in the league?

636. What was the score of the game in Q635?

637. Can you recall the opposition when Raimond Van Der Gouw made his first start of the season?

638. What injury kept Peter Schmeichel out of the game in Q637, a gashed shin, a stomach strain or a slight cold?

639. Against what London club did Dwight Yorke make his Manchester United debut?

640. Dwight Yorke scored on his Old Trafford debut. Name United's capital opponents.

SCOTLAND UNITED

641. How many international caps did Gordon McQueen win - 30, 40 or 50?

642. What is Paddy Crerand's middle name - Christopher, Damien or Timothy?

643. Name either of the two league clubs that Tommy Docherty both played for and managed.

644. How many FA Cup goals did Denis Law score for Manchester United - 31, 34 or 38?

645. Name the Manchester United striker who won the Manchester United Members' Player of the Year Award in 1988?

646. Can you name the former United defender who owned a bar in Coventry named The Rising Sun after his football career ended?

647. Which World Cup Finals did Arthur Albiston participate in for Scotland?

648. Name the former Reds captain who was appointed Chairman of the Manchester United Fan Club in 1973?

649. How many caps did David Herd win - 5, 10 or 15?

650. In what year did Gordon McQueen win an FA Cup winners' medal with United?

TRIVIA - 9

651. What was the most number of league goals scored by Nobby Stiles in a single season during his United career - 7, 8 or 9?

652. What Scottish club did Jim Leighton join when he left United?

653. Did George Best coach the National Team of China, Japan or Malaysia?

654. Can you recall the name of the Russian side which United played in the 1986 Amsterdam 711 Tournament?

655. Name the United goalkeeper who hit the Liverpool crossbar when the Reds visited Anfield on 26 December 1979.

656. When Old Trafford had floodlights installed in 1957 did they cost £40,000, £50,0000 or £60,000?

657. In what year was Manchester United's Membership Scheme introduced?

658. Which one of the Greenhoff brothers made the most appearances for United, Brian or Jimmy?

659. During the 1980's how many times did United finish outside the Top 10 of the First Division?

660. True or False, Gordon McQueen played in the 1985 FA Cup Final for United against Everton?

WALES UNITED

661. During season 1984-1985 how many hat-tricks did Mark Hughes score for United?

662. Can you name the Manchester City player who joined United in September 1972?

663. On their way to winning the European Cup Winners' Cup in 1991 how many goals did Clayton Blackmore score in the competition - 2, 3 or 4?

664. In what year did Ryan Giggs win the Professional Footballers' Association Young Player Of The Year Award?

665. True or False, Alan Davies was actually born in Manchester.

666. When Alan Davies left Old Trafford which North East team did he sign for?

667. When Mark Hughes left Stamford Bridge which club did he join?

668. Against what Polish side did Ryan Giggs score his first goal of the 1998-1999 season?

669. In what year did Jimmy Murphy lead United out at Wembley for the FA Cup Final?

670. How many FA Cup winners' medals did Billy Meredith win during his career?

IRELAND UNITED

671. How many seasons did George Best play all 42 league games for Manchester United?

672. Who became United's youngest captain since the war when he captained the side in 1983?

673. Name the Reds' striker who captained the Republic of Ireland team in their 8-0 win over Malta in 1983.

674. During his Old Trafford career Johnny Giles won only one major winners' medal. In what competition did the Reds triumph?

675. What brand of sausages did George Best advertise during the 1970's?

676. In what city was Kevin Moran born - Cork, Dublin or Galway?

677. What club, beginning with the letter B, did Paddy Roche join in 1982?

678. Name the Irish player, whose surname is a country in South America, who made his league debut for the Reds in 1989.

679. During season 1966-1967 George Best wore 2 different shirt numbers for United. What were they?

680. Against which Midlands club did Ashley Grimes make his Manchester United debut?

FA CUP - 2

681. True or False, on their way to winning the 1909 FA Cup United met Manchester City in the 3rd Round?

682. Which Yorkshire club put the Reds United out of the 1914-1915 competition?

683. United beat Aston Villa in their 3rd Round tie on 10 January 1948 at Villa Park. What was the score of the game, 4-3, 5-2 or 6-4?

684. Can you recall the Irish player who made his debut for the club in the famous 5th Round tie just thirteen days after the Munich Air Disaster?

685. How many goals did the player in no. 684 score in the above 5th Round game?

686. In what year did United play their first FA Cup Final at Wembley?

687. Name the London club which put United out of the 1967-1968 competition after a Replay.

688. Why did the Football Association order the making of a new FA Cup after United's 1909 success?

689. In the 1980-1981 competition United met a team that they would later play in an FA Cup Final during the 1980's. Name the team.

690. United met the same opponents in the 3rd Round of the 1983 1984 competition that they met in the 3rd Round in 1984-1985. Can you name the seaside team involved?

GUESS MY NAME - 2

691.   I was born in Reading and joined United from Nottingham
       Forest. I won an FA Cup winners' medal with the Reds in 1990,
       a European Cup Winners' Cup winners' medal & a European
       Super Cup winners' medal in 1991.

692.   I was born in Aberdeen. During my career I played for
       Manchester City and I also played abroad. In 1963 I won an FA
       Cup winners' medal with United after scoring in the Final.

693.   I was born in Salford on 1st November 1956. I was a member of
       the famous Busby Babes and won three FA Youth Cup winners'
       medals in 1953, 1954 & 1955. I died in the Munich Air Disaster.

694.   I joined United from Leeds United in 1978 and when I left Old
       Trafford in 1985 I joined the Seiko club in Hong Kong.

695.   Tommy Docherty brought me to Old Trafford in 1974. With
       United I won a Second Division Championship winners' medal
       in 1975 and an FA Cup winners' medal in 1977. In 1981 I made
       my 200th consecutive appearance for the Reds.

696.   I am a goalkeeper and joined United from Sunderland in 1985.
       After leaving Old Trafford I moved to Sheffield Wednesday.

697.   I was purchased by Matt Busby in 1963 from Glasgow Celtic. I
       was assistant manager to Tommy Docherty and also had a brief
       managerial spell at Northampton Town.

698.   I was born in Leicester and cost the Reds £1million in 1992.
       During my career I have also played for Coventry City & Aston
       Villa.

699. I cost United a record £2.3million for a defender when Alex Ferguson purchased me. After leaving Old Trafford I joined one of my former clubs.

700. I scored my first goal for United against Chelsea on 19th December 1992.

NAME THE TEAM - 7

The 1990 FA Cup Winning Team

1.   L-------S-----------

2.   P--------I------

3.   L------M---------

4.   S-------B--------

5.   M------P--------

6.   G------P--------

7.   B---------R-------

8.   N-------W-------

9.   B-------M-------

10.   M-------H----------

11.   D------W-------

NUMBER 1 HITS

All you have to do here is associate the event with the record which was at No. 1 in the UK charts at the time.

701. World Club Championship Runners-Up — Seasons In The Sun by Terry Jacks

702. United are relegated to Division 2 — Don't Leave Me This Way by The Communards

703. Eric Cantona's debut — I Don't Wanna Talk About It by Rod Stewart

704. Premier League Champions — Give It Up by KC & The Sunshine Band

705. Alex Ferguson takes charge — Young Girl by Union Gap featuring Gary Puckett

706. European Cup Winners' Cup Winners — Those Were The Days by Mary Hopkin

707. FA Charity Shield Winners — Shoop Shoop Song by Cher

708. European Super Cup Winners — Five Live EP by George Michael & Queen With Lisa Stansfield

709. FA Cup Winners — Dizzy by Vic Reeves & The Wonder Stuff

710. European Cup Winners — I Will Always Love You by Whitney Houston

TRANSFER PRICES

*All you have to do here is associate the player with the amount
of money United received for him following his transfer.*

711.	Ted MacDougall	to West Ham United	£45,000
712.	Carlo Satori	to Bologna	£50,000
713.	Ray O'Brien	to Notts County	£220,000
714.	Brian Kidd	to Arsenal	£40,000
715.	Jim McCalliog	to Southampton	£250,000
716.	Jim Holton	to Sunderland	£170,000
717.	Gerry Daly	to Derby County	£40,000
718.	Gordon Hill	to Derby County	£110,000
719.	Jonathan Clark	to Derby County	£64,000
720.	Stuart Pearson	to West Ham United	£175,000

NEWTON HEATH - 2

721. What have Harry Stafford, William Morgan and Alfred Schofield all got in common?

722. Was Fred Erentz born in Aberdeen, Bellshill or Dundee?

723. What team, beginning with the letter C, were Newton Heath's last opponents in the Football League?

724. In what Division of the Football League were Newton Heath when they became Manchester United?

725. What was their final season of existence 1899-00, 1900-01 or 1901-02?

726. In what position did Newton Heath finish in their final season in the Football League - 11th, 13th or 15th?

727. True or False, Newton Heath never played Manchester City in a Division 2 game?

728. Can you name Newton Heath's manager who led them from the Football Alliance into the Football League?

729. Name the last team, with the initials L C, that Newton Heath played in an FA Cup tie.

730. True or False, Harry Stafford played for Newton Heath in both the 19th & 20th century?

TRIVIA - 10

731.   True or False, United's Charlie Mitten was born in Rangoon, Burma?

732.   How many goals did Mal Donaghy score for Manchester United?

733.   Name the two Argentina international forwards which United were reportedly interested in signing in May 1998.

734.   What number of shirt did David Beckham wear in the 1996 FA Cup Final?

735.   What award did Mark Hughes win in 1989?

736.   Name the future United star who scored for their Youth Team against Swindon Town in the 1963-64 FA Youth Cup Final, 1st Leg.

737.   Two United players played for England against Italy in 1989. Bryan Robson was one, can you name the other?

738.   What shirt number did Denis Law wear in the 1968 European Cup Final?

739.   True or False, Ryan Giggs played in United's 1991 European Super Cup winning team?

740.   Name the former Manchester United player who was part of ITV's 1974 World Cup Final panel.

UNITED AT THE WORLD CUP FINALS - 1

741. Can you name two of the three Manchester United players who were in the England World Cup squad at Mexico 1986?

742. How many games did United's Colin Webster play for Wales in the 1958 Finals in Sweden 3, 4 or 5?

743. Who was the first Manchester United player to play for his country at a World Cup Final tournament (i.e. the Finals as opposed to the Final itself)?

744. Name the England defender who was in their 1990 World Cup Final squad and who later joined Manchester United from a London club.

745. Apart from Martin Buchan, which other United defender played in the 1974 World Cup Finals?

746. At which World Cup Finals did the Reds' Willie Morgan represent Scotland?

747. Bryan Robson, Ray Wilkins and which other Manchester United player were in the England squad for the 1982 Finals in Spain?

748. How many Manchester United players represented their country at the 1958 Finals?

749. Can you name the United defender who played for Scotland at the 1978 Finals in Argentina?

750. Name 2 of the 3 Manchester United players who were in the England squad at the 1970 Finals in Mexico.

LEGENDS - 4

751. Name the Manchester United striker who scored their last goal in a Division 1 league game.

752. Can you recall the Brisbane based Australian football team which George Best played for?

753. Who was the first £200,000 player purchased by Manchester United?

754. Apart from Millwall, what other London based club did Gordon Hill play for?

755. Which Yorkshire club did Frank Stapleton once join as Player Manager?

756. One of the Greenhoff brothers managed Toronto Blizzard in Canada. Was it Brian or Jimmy?

757. Who scored United's first ever goal in the FA Premier League?

758. Name 2 of the 4 City's ex-Red, Gerry Daly, played for.

759. From which Scottish league side did Manchester United purchase Alex Forsyth?

760. United beat Blackpool 4-0 on the final day of the 1974-75 Division 2 Championship winning season. Name 2 of the 3 United forwards who were the last players to score for the club in an English League Division 2 game.

LEGEND - WILF McGUINNESS

761.   In what year did Wilf join United - 1951, 1952 or 1953?

762.   Against what Midlands club did Wilf make his debut for United?

763.   In what year was Wilf appointed the manager of Manchester United?

764.   Who did Wilf replace as the United manager?

765.   What was the first trophy Wilf won with United?

766.   What type of injury forced Wilf to retire from playing Professional football aged only 22?

767.   What Team was Wilf the Trainer of from 1963-1969?

768.   Name either 1 of the 2 Greek teams Wilf managed.

769.   Can you recall the City that Wilf was appointed the manager of in 1975?

770.   To the nearest 10, how many games in total did Wilf play for United?

MIXED BAG - 2

771. Can you name the side which finished Runners-Up to United in season 1964-65 just one year after they won the Second Division Championship?

772. Who did former Reds boss, Ron Atkinson, describe as the best player in the world - Cruyff, Maradona or Pele?

773. Name the former Manchester United assistant manager who became Walter Smith's right hand man at Everton at the start of the 1998-99 season.

774. A former Manchester United player managed Oldham Athletic when they played Chelsea in the FA Cup 3rd Round on 2 January 1999. Name him.

775. Brian Kidd left Old Trafford at the end of 1998 to take up the vacant manager's job at which club?

776. Which former United star did Brian Kidd appoint as his assistant manager at the club in Q775?

777. Name the former United winger who Brian Kidd made his first signing when he took up his appointment in Q775.

778. How many FA Youth Cup Finals did Manchester United participate in during the 1980's?

779. Adidas made United's 1991 European Cup Winners' Cup shirt but which sponsors name appeared across the body of it?

780. Alex Stepney cost United a world record fee for a goalkeeper in 1966. Did he cost the Reds £55,000, £75,000 or £105,000?

RE-ARRANGE THE TEAM

The following are all teams Manchester United have played. All you have to do here is re-arrange the team in order that it reads properly.

781.	Raba Vasas	Select
782.	Red Star	Roma
783.	Gornik	Kickers
784.	Grantham	1896
785.	New York	Volgograd
786.	Bradford Park	ETO
787.	Stuttgart	Town
788.	Hannover	Belgrade
789.	Rotor	Avenue
790.	Tevere	Zagreb

TRIVIA - 11

791. Between Dave Sexton's sacking and Ron Atkinson's appointment, a former United goalkeeper assumed the role of Assistant Manager at Old Trafford. Name him.

792. Who was the manager of Scotland when Alex Ferguson held the post of Assistant Manager?

793. True or False, Manchester United did not have a manager between 1937-45.

794. When George Best played for the San Jose Earthquakes in 1981 one of his former team mates managed the side. Name the player in question.

795. Can you name the Premier League forward who was sent off after a confrontation with Peter Schmeichel in April 1993 only for his dismissal to be later overturned?

796. For what reason did Alex Ferguson face disciplinary action by the Football Association in 1993?

797. During the 1970-71 season United's matchday programme, United Review, had the price on the front cover. Why?

798. Can you recall the name of the Reds' manager when Alex Stepney left the club?

799. Against what London club did United wear their new all-black kit for the first time during the 1998-99 season?

800. Can you name the Manchester United player who came on as a substitute versus Southampton on 3 October 1998 and scored?

NAME THE TEAM - 8

The 1991 European Super Cup Winning Team

1.   P--------S-----------

2.   D------I---------

3.   L-------M--------

4.   S------B---------

5.   N------W--------

6.   G-----P---------

7.   A-----K----------

8.   P-----I-------

9.   B-------M-------

10.   M-------H-----------

11.   C-------B--------

DEBUTS - 1

All you have to do here is match the player with the team he made his Manchester United debut against.

801. George Graham   Sheffield Wednesday

802. Harry Gregg   Aston Villa

803. Dion Dublin   Middlesbrough

804. Brian Kidd   Leicester City

805. Billy Meredith   Arsenal

806. David Sadler   Wolverhampton Wanderers

807. Denis Law   Southampton

808. Martin Buchan   West Bromwich Albion

809. Wilf McGuinness   Everton

810. Remi Moses   Tottenham Hotspur

THE 1970's - 2

811.   In season 1972-73 United bought two players from Irish side, Bohemians. Name either of them.

812.   How many different managers did Manchester United have during the 1970's?

813.   Which Lancashire club did United sell winger, Willie Morgan, to during the 1975-76 season?

814.   Can you name the Midlands club that defeated the Reds in the Semi-Final of the 1970-71 Football League Cup?

815.   What was the first season during the decade that saw the Reds participating in a European competition?

816.   Name the manager of Manchester United when FC Porto put them out of the European Cup Winners' Cup in season 1977-78.

817.   Can you recall the United player who made his International debut for England against Northern Ireland in 1970?

818.   In what year during the decade were the Reds defeated in the Semi-Final of the FA Cup by Leeds United?

819.   In season 1971-72 United paid Nottingham Forest £200,000 for a striker. Name the player concerned.

820.   How many FA Charity Shields did the Reds compete for during the 1970's?

SEASON 1998-1999 - 3

821.   The kick-off time for the Manchester United versus West Ham United game played on Sunday 10th January was delayed by 45 minutes. Why?

822.   In the game in Q821 there were two players on the pitch with the same surname. Name them.

823.   Can you name United's substitute goalkeeper who was on the bench for the West Ham United game at Old Trafford?

824.   United entertained Middlesbrough in the 3rd Round of the FA Cup at Old Trafford. Three former United players formed the management team for the visitors. Name them.

825.   Can you name the former Manchester United player who was named the Carling Manager of the Month for December?

826.   Against which team did Jesper Blomqvist score his first goal for the Reds?

827.   In what Round of the Worthington League Cup were United eliminated?

828.   Name the side which ended United's Worthington League Cup hopes.

829.   Who played his first League Cup game for three years when he played in the game in Q828?

830.   Can you name the Scottish Premier League side which United played in a friendly on 18 January?

UEFA CHAMPIONS LEAGUE
1998-1999

831.   Name the Polish side which United defeated in their Champions
        League Qualifying game.

832.   Name two of the three clubs which formed United's Group.

833.   Which Group were the Reds drawn to play in - B, D or F?

834.   When United met Bayern Munich in the Olympic Stadium a
        Brazilian scored for the Germans. Name him.

835.   Name the United midfielder who was sent off in one of United's
        Group games at Old Trafford.

836.   Who were United's opponents and what was the score of the
        game in Q835?

837.   Who were the first club United scored an away goal against in the
        competition?

838.   What was the score of the United versus Bayern Munich game at
        Old Trafford?

839.   How many points did the Reds finish with in their Group?

840.   United created Champions League history by scoring the most
        goals ever in the Group stages. How many goals did they score
        in their 6 Group games?

WINNERS

All you have to do here is associate the Trophy with the year Manchester United won it.

841.	FA Cup	1991
842.	FA Charity Shield	1936
843.	FA Youth Cup	1969
844.	Lancashire FA Youth Cup	1909
845.	Football League Division 1	1955
846.	Central League	1993
847.	Lancashire FA Senior Cup	1964
848.	Manchester FA Senior Cup	1952
849.	Football League Cup	1960
850.	Football League Division 2	1992

TAKE IT AS WORN

851. Can you recall the year which first saw United wear the SHARP logo on their shirts?

852. At the beginning of the 1994-95 season United introduced a new home jersey. What was unusual about the design of the shirt?

853. What colour of socks did Alex Stepney wear in the 1968 European Cup Final?

854. United introduced a new 3rd kit in December 1994. What colour was the shirt?

855. Apart from SHARP and the manufacturers' logo, UMBRO, what else was written on the shirt in Q854?

856. What colour of shirt did United wear when they played in their first FA Cup Final in 1909?

857. Can you describe the feature of the badge on the shirt in Q856?

858. True or False, United wore a Red Shamrock on their shirts between 1910-14?

859. United met Liverpool in the 1983 League Cup Final at Wembley. What colour of shirt & shorts did United wear?

860. What was unusual about the colour of shirts worn by the players of Manchester United and Blackpool in the 1948 FA Cup Final?

BIG RON

861. In what year did Ron Atkinson become the manager of Manchester United?

862. What is Ron Atkinson's middle name - Frederick, Lawrence or Robert?

863. Name the non-league side where he started his managerial career.

864. Shortly after Ron Atkinson arrived at Old Trafford two former United goalkeepers, who were coaches prior to his appointment as manager, left the club. Name either of them.

865. Who did Ron Atkinson succeed as manager of Manchester United?

866. Can you name Ron Atkinson's assistant-manager at West Bromwich Albion who he later persuaded to join him at Old Trafford?

867. Can you recall the first player Ron Atkinson purchased for Manchester United?

868. Name the Scottish player who scored United's first league goal under Ron Atkinson.

869. What was the first trophy United won under Ron Atkinson?

870. Towards the end of 1998 Ron Atkinson had a book published. What is the title of the book?

UNITED INTERNATIONALS - 2

All you have to do here is associate the United player with the country he made his International debut against.

871.	Johnny Berry	Sweden
872.	Bill Foulkes	Turkey
873.	David Pegg	Wales
874.	Nobby Stiles	Argentina
875.	Alex Stepney	Israel
876.	Jim Holton	Eire
877.	George Best	England
878.	Jimmy Nicholl	USSR
879.	Paddy Roche	Northern Ireland
880.	Ashley Grimes	Scotland

FA CUP - 3

881. Can you name the full-back who Mike Duxbury came on as a substitute for in the 1985 FA Cup Final?

882. What shirt number did Andy Cole wear in the 1996 Final?

883. Which Premier League side did the Reds defeat in the 3rd Round on 3 January 1999?

884. Name the Lancashire side who put United, the Cup holders, out of the 1909-10 competition.

885. Who was Manchester United's top goalscorer in their successful 1948 FA Cup run?

886. Name either of United's 2 goalscorers in their 1991-92 4th Round Replay draw with Southampton at Old Trafford.

887. Who scored the Reds' last goal in the 1997-98 competition?

888. Can you name either of the two London based teams which United met in the 1987-1988 competition?

889. Name the player who scored United's third goal in their 3-3 draw with Oldham Athletic at Maine Road in 1989-90.

890. Name either of the Reds' two substitutes who came on in the 1994 Final.

SIR MATT BUSBY

891. When Sir Matt retired in 1969 he took up a new position at Old Trafford. What was the title given to his new post?

892. In what year did a young Matt Busby become the manager of Manchester United?

893. True or False, Matt Busby played for Manchester United before the outbreak of World War II?

894. During his managerial career at Old Trafford Matt Busby was ably assisted by a Welshman. Can you name the man who was his assistant-manager?

895. Who was the most expensive player Matt Busby purchased - Denis Law, Albert Quixall or Alex Stepney?

896. In 1936 Matt Busby signed for Liverpool. Did he cost the Merseyside club £6,000, £8,000 or £10,000?

897. In what year was he made a Freeman of the City of Manchester?

898. Can you recall the year in which the Great Man died?

899. How many First Division Championships did United win during his reign as manager?

900. From which Scottish club did he sign Jimmy Delaney shortly after he took up the job as United manager?

NAME THE TEAM - 9

The 1985 FA Cup Winning Team

1.   G--------B-----------

2.   J--------G-------

3.   A-------A--------

4.   N-------W--------

5.   P------M--------

6.   K------M--------

7.   B-------R-------

8.   G------S--------

9.   F-------S---------

10.   M------H-----------

11.   J-------O---------

PREMIER LEAGUE FIRSTS

From the following clue all you have to do is match the event with the team. All events took place in the FA Carling Premier League.

901.	The first team to beat United	Everton
902.	The first team United drew with.	Sheffield United
903.	The first team United scored against	Crystal Palace
904.	The first team to score against United at Old Trafford	Southampton
905.	The first team United beat	Nottingham Forest
906.	The first team United beat at Old Trafford	Sheffield United
907.	The first team United beat away.	Ipswich Town
908.	The first team United scored against at Old Trafford	Chelsea
909.	The first team United beat twice	Southampton
910.	The first team to beat United twice	Ipswich Town

DEBUTS - 2

All you have to do here is match the player with the team he made his Manchester United debut against.

911.	Ray Wood	Manchester City
912.	Gordon McQueen	Tottenham Hotspur
913.	Denis Irwin	Oldham Athletic
914.	Mickey Thomas	West Ham United
915.	Ben Thornley	Leicester City
916.	Bryan Robson	Grimsby Town
917.	Nicky Butt	Coventry City
918.	Jimmy Delaney	Liverpool
919.	Alex Stepney	Newcastle United
920.	Jimmy Greenhoff	Chelsea

LEADING GOALSCORERS

All you have to do here is associate the United player with the season in which he finished as United's Leading Goalscorer.

921.	George Best	1984-1985
922.	Bobby Charlton	1962-1963
923.	David Herd	1977-1978
924.	Gordon Hill	1958-1959
925.	Mark Hughes	1979-1980
926.	Joe Jordan	1967-1968
927.	Denis Law	1975-1976
928.	Lou Macari	1959-1960
929.	Frank Stapleton	1961-1962
930.	Dennis Viollet	1983-1984

THE OPPOSITION

931. Can you name the Tottenham Hotspur player who scored 4 goals against United at Old Trafford on 28 October 1972?

932. Name the team that knocked United out of the 1984-85 UEFA Cup in a penalty shoot-out.

933. How many times did the Reds meet Stoke City during the 1971-72 season 4, 5 or 7?

934. Name the Yorkshire side which defeated United 6-0 at Old Trafford in a Division 1 game on 10 September 1930.

935. In March 1999 Dwight Yorke scored United's 100th goal of the season. Who were the Reds' opponents?

936. In the 1964-65 Inter-Cities Fairs Cup United played a French League side. Can you name them?

937. Who were United's first Italian opponents in a European Cup tie?

938. Name the London club United met in both the League Cup and FA Cup during the 1985-86 season.

939. Against which Portuguese team did Denis Law score a hat-trick in a European Cup Winners' Cup Quarter-Final tie at Old Trafford on 26 February 1964?

940. The Reds have met 2 English sides in European competition. Name the first English side they met.

UNITED DEFENDERS

941. In his first season with United Denis Irwin won a Cup winners' medal. Name the Cup competition concerned.

942. Name the former Everton defender who won an FA Cup winners' medal with United during the 1980's.

943. Did Roger Byrne play left-back or right back for Manchester United & England?

944. In what year did Gary Pallister make his International debut for England?

945. A Reds' defender played for a The Rest Of The World side against England in 1987. Name him.

946. Only one player of the 1992-1993 FA Carling Premier League winning team was not capped by his country. Can you name him?

947. Name the full-back who broke his ankle against Bristol City and therefore missed the 1977 FA Cup Final.

948. Can you name the United defender who played in all 6 of United's Champions League games during the 1994-1995 season?

949. Who scored United's goal in their 1-1 draw with Crystal Palace in January 1995, a match which will always be remembered for Eric Cantona's sending off?

950. A Manchester United defender left the club in August 1988 to play in Spain for Sporting Gijon. Name him.

UNITED FRONTMEN

951.   Can you name the 'David' Matt Busby paid Arsenal £35,000 for in July 1961?

952.   How many FA Cup winners medals did Stuart Pearson win during his career?

953.   For which company did Eric Cantona model clothes for in Paris in December 1992?

954.   Did Lee Sharpe make his England International debut against Northern Ireland or the Republic of Ireland?

955.   Can you recall the Spurs striker who Andy Cole came on for when he made his debut for England versus Uruguay?

956.   Name the striker who scored the Reds' winner in their 2-1 FA Carling Premier League victory over Liverpool at Anfield in March 1993.

957.   Mark Hughes was suspended for an important World Cup match in November 1993. Can you recall the country Wales played?

958.   What did Lee Sharpe use as a microphone to celebrate his goal against Queens Park Rangers in an FA Cup Quarter-Final tie at Old Trafford in March 19995?

959.   Was Jimmy Greenhoff's FA Cup Semi-Final winning goal against Liverpool in 1979 a header, a penalty or a volley?

960.   Name either of the two outfield players who were on the bench for the 1995 FA Cup Final against Everton.

THE 1980's - 2

961.   When English clubs were banned from European Competitions during the 1980's a new Cup Competition was created in England. Name the Cup concerned.

962.   In what season was the Cup in Q961 first competed for?

963.   United were beaten 1-0 in the 3rd Round of the FA Cup at Old Trafford in January 1980. The only goal of the game was scored by a player who held a World Cup Winners' medal. Name the player concerned.

964.   Can you name the Birmingham City striker who Ron Atkinson attempted to sign in 1981 only for the player to join Leeds United instead?

965.   When Bryan Robson joined the Reds another West Bromwich Albion player also moved to Old Trafford in the deal. Name him.

966.   Under Ron Atkinson's first full season in charge of United did the Reds finish the season in 2nd, 3rd or 4th place in Division 1?

967.   Name the club United defeated 4-0 at Old Trafford in the Quarter-Final of the 1982-83 League Cup.

968.   Can you name the London club which defeated United 2-1 in the Final of the Football Association Centenary Trophy on 9th October 1988?

969.   At which Midlands Ground was the Final in Q968 played?

970.   Name the United forward who scored a hat-trick against Rotherham in the Reds' 5-0 League Cup Round 2, 2nd leg win at Old Trafford in October 1988.

TRIVIA - 12

971.   Can you name the on-loan United player who scored for Manchester City in their 3-0 Division 2 win over Millwall at Maine Road on 6 February 1999?

972.   Ryan Giggs pulled his hamstring in a Premier League game on 3 February 1999. He also damaged his hamstring against the same opponents the previous season. Who were the Reds' opponents?

973.   Which former Manchester United manager was nicknamed The Tank during his playing career?

974.   Against what City did Dwight Yorke score a hat-trick for the Reds on 16 January 1999?

975.   What was the score of the game in Q974?

976.   Can you name the United defender who scored his first goal for the club in the game in Q974?

977.   Who captained the Reds in their Champions League game against Bayern Munich [away] on 9 December 1998?

978.   Name the United player who passed the ball to Michael Owen before the Liverpool player scored his superb goal against Argentina at the World Cup in France in June 1998.

979.   Who was in charge of team affairs for the Reds' home game against Middlesbrough at Old Trafford on 19 December 1998?

980.   True or False, United finished Runners-Up to Liverpool in season 1976-1977?

LEGEND - PETER SCHMEICHEL

981.   How much did United pay Brondby for his services?

982.   What European Award did he win in 1995?

983.   In what year was Peter Schmeichel voted the FA Carling Premier League Player Of The Year?

984.   During what season did Peter score his first and only goal for the Reds?

985.   True or False, he captained Denmark to European Championship success in 1992?

986.   Can you name the goalkeeper who Peter succeeded in goal for Manchester United?

987.   In what year was Peter voted the FA Premier League Goalkeeper of The Year 1993 or 1995?

988.   Name the Juventus player who scored against Peter in the 1-1 draw at Old Trafford in the 1st leg of their UEFA Champions League Semi-Final clash.

989.   Peter Schmeichel is the joint-record holder for keeping the most number of clean sheets in goal for the Reds. Which other United legend does he share the record with?

990.   Who were the opposition when he played his last competitive game for United?

NAME THE TEAM - 10

The 1991 European Cup Winners' Cup Winning Team

1.   L-------S-----------

2.   D-------I------

3.   C------B---------

4.   S-------B-------

5.   M-------P-------

6.   G------P--------

7.   B-------R--------

8.   P------I--------

9.   B------M----------

10.   M--------H---------

11.   L------S---------

MIXED BAG - 3

991. A manager of a Premier League side during the 1998-1999 season was Alex Ferguson's assistant manager of the Scotland team at the 1986 World Cup Finals. Name him.

992. From which City did the Reds sign goalkeeper, Nick Culkin?

993. Who scored United's equaliser against Inter Milan in the San Siro Stadium in March 1999?

994. Which one of the Neville brothers did Alex Ferguson include in his all-star United Dream Team?

995. In February 1999 United signed 17 year-old Bojan Djordic. What nationality is Bojan?

996. Name the former United striker who joined Manchester City on loan from Greek side, Panionios, on 25 March 1999.

997. How many England managers has Gary Neville played under?

998. Can you name the Red Devil who got married in February 1999?

999. What City did Philip Mulryne sign for when he left Old Trafford on the transfer deadline date of 25 March 1999?

1000. Four past and present United players played in the England v Czech Republic friendly at Wembley on 18 November 1998. Name 3 of them.

TRIVIA - 13

1001. Bobby Charlton scored four hat-tricks for England. Name any one of the four countries who were on the receiving end.

1002. When Roy Keane was substituted in United's FA Premier League 8-1 win at Nottingham Forest on 6 February 1999 who took over the captain's armband for the last twenty minutes?

1003. Which former Red scored the first hat-trick of his career in an FA Premier League game at Old Trafford on 10 November 1994?

1004. Name 2 of the 3 United players who were short-listed for the 1999 PFA Player of the Year Award.

1005. When the Reds won the 1999 UEFA Champions League how many games during the season did their unbeaten run extend to?

1006. When UEFA handed over the European Cup to the Mayor of Barcelona prior to the 1999 Final a representative from past Manchester United and Bayern Munich sides attended the cermony. Can you name the 1968 European Cup winning defender who represented United?

1007. Who were United's London opponents in Brian Kidd's last game as Assistant-Manager?

1008. Only one team prevented the Reds from scoring in the 1999 UEFA Champions League competition. Name them.

1009. Did Denis Law score more goals for United in the FA Cup, European competitions or League Cup?

1010. Name the United defender who was sent off in a Premier League game on 12 December 1998.

LEGENDS - 5

1011. Can you name the United midfielder of the 1980's, who in 1999 was managing a Roller-Hockey team named The Warriors from Middleton?

1012. Name the United manager who signed Mickey Thomas from Wrexham.

1013. Who was the United defender who played in England's 2-0 win over Brazil in a friendly in June 1984?

1014. Did United's Assistant Coach, Jim Ryan, play alongside Alex Stepney, Paddy Roche or Gary Bailey in the USA for the Dallas Tornados?

1015. Name the former United player who was substituted in the 1982 European Cup Final.

1016. Did Johnny Carey play more games for Northern Ireland or the Republic of Ireland?

1017. Can you name the Reds' defender who was the only ever present member of Manchester United's 1951-1952 Championship winning team?

1018. Name the goalkeeper United signed and upon joining the Reds commanded the first ever 5 figure transfer fee.

1019. Name the former United player Jack Charlton slated in his autobiography, Jack Charlton - The Autobiography, in the chapter about the World Cup in Italia '90.

1020. Who was the United player who played for Wales at the World Cup Finals in Sweden in 1958?

OLD TRAFFORD

1021. Old Trafford staged an FA Cup Semi-Final tie on 22 March 1950. Name either of the two teams involved.

1022. The record attendance for Old Trafford was set in March 1939 when the ground was used to stage an FA Cup Semi-Final. How many were in attendance - 69,947, 76,892 or 81,109?

1023. Name either of the two teams that played in the game in Q1022.

1024. What country did England defeat 7-0 at Old Trafford in an International Match on 16 November 1938?

1025. Which Championship game did Old Trafford host on 16 October 1968?

1026. Can you name England's opponents at Old Trafford on 22 November 1997?

1027. In what month and year was Old Trafford demolished in a German bombing raid during World War 2?

1028. Name the first team to play a league game at Old Trafford after the Munich Air Disaster.

1029. What nickname was given to the 1915 FA Cup Final which was played at Old Trafford?

1030. In what year was Old Trafford officially opened?

STRIKE FORCE

1031. What was significant about Frank Stapleton's hat-trick for United against Watford at Old Trafford on 19 November 1983?

1032. When Ryan Giggs made his league debut for the Reds, what number of shirt did he wear?

1033. What was Terry Gibson's officially registered height during his spell at Old Trafford?

1034. Can you name the United winger who was a guest on A Question of Sport in March 1986?

1035. Who was top goalscorer for the Reds in seasons 1946-47 - 1949-50 inclusive?

1036. Name the city that both Joe Jordan and Lou Macari have managed.

1037. Andy Cole was voted FA Carling Player of the Month for November 1997 along with a Southampton forward. Name the striker.

1038. In what year during the 1980's did Steve Coppell win his last cap for England?

1039. Which former Old Trafford Scottish hero's family originated from Rome, Italy?

1040. What number of shirt did Mark Hughes wear in the 1985 FA Cup Final?

UNITED v CITY

1041. During the 1960's United only won both Derby games in the same season on two occasions. Name either season.

1042. True or False, the Reds lost both Derby games in season 1969-70?

1043. How many Manchester Derbies did United win under the reign of Frank O'Farrell?

1044. In which season during the 1950's did the Reds lose both Derby games?

1045. What was the score of the Derby game at Old Trafford on 12 February 1955?

1046. Can you recall the year during the 1980's that United's Youth Team lost to City's Youth Team in the FA Youth Cup Final?

1047. True or False, United won both Derby games during season 1976-77?

1048. Who scored a hat-trick for City in the Derby game at Old Trafford on 12 December 1970?

1049. Name the striker who scored United's 100th goal in Derby games.

1050. United and City drew 2-2 at Old Trafford on 22 March 1986. Which United ful-back scored an own-goal that day?

LEGEND - ERIC CANTONA - 2

1051.   Eric scored a penalty at Wembley in August 1994. Who were United's opponents?

1052.   True or False, Eric captained United to FA Cup success over Chelsea in 1994?

1053.   What was unusual about Eric's sending off in United's European Cup game away to Galatasaray on 3 November 1993?

1054.   What was Eric's profession in the 1997 film A Question Of Honour?

1055.   In September 1997 Eric played in a Beach Soccer Tournament in Monaco. Whose team did he represent?

1056.   How many penalties did Eric score during the 1995-96 season - 5, 8 or 11?

1057.   Can you name either of the two French league clubs where Eric had two different spells with?

1058.   Name the former French National Team Manager with whom Eric had a bust-up during the time Eric played for Olympique Marseille.

1059.   In his first season at Old Trafford did Eric score 9, 14, or 19 goals in the Premier League?

1060.   Which Premier League club made an audacious £4million bid for Eric in July 1996?

MOVING ON - 2

*All you have to do here is match the United player with the club
he joined when he left Old Trafford.*

1061.	Harry Gregg	Everton
1062.	Lee Sharpe	Sheffield Wednesday
1063.	David Sadler	Glasgow Celtic
1064.	Norman Whiteside	Ajax Amsterdam
1065.	Chris Turner	Stoke City
1066.	Frank Stapleton	Crewe Alexandria
1067.	Dion Dublin	Miami Tornados
1068.	Jimmy Greenhoff	Everton
1069.	Lee Martin	Coventry City
1070.	Mickey Thomas	Leeds United

WHERE WAS I BORN?

All you have to do here is match the player with his place of birth.

1071.	Denis Law	Ayr
1072.	Steve Bruce	West Ham
1073.	Bobby Charlton	Manchester
1074.	Stuart Pearson	Aberdeen
1075.	Viv Anderson	Cork
1076.	Clayton Blackmore	Hull
1077.	Paul Parker	Ashington
1078.	Shay Brennan	Corbridge
1079.	Ian Ure	Nottingham
1080.	Roy Keane	Neath

NAME THE TEAM - 11

The 2004 FA Cup Winning Team

14.   T-------H-----------

2.   G-------N------

25.   J-------O-------

27.   M------S--------

6.   W------B---------

7.   C-------R--------

16.   R-------K-------

24.   D------F--------

11.   R-------G--------

18.   P------S----------

10.   R---------V---------

KEANO

1081.   Where in Ireland was Roy born?

1082.   At what Irish club did Roy begin his career?

1083.   True or False, Keano was sent off in his first game as Captain of the Republic of Ireland?

1084.   Can you name the former Republic of Ireland manager that Roy had a major disagreement with prior to the 2002 World Cup Finals?

1085.   Roy made his United league debut on the opening day of the 1993-94 season. What team did United beat 2-0?

1086.   From what club did United sign Roy?

1087.   To the nearest £250,000 how much did United pay for Roy?

1088.   Who did Roy take over the captaincy of United from?

1089.   What was the first trophy Roy won with United?

1090.   Can you recall the 1999 Final in which Roy scored the winning goal?

GOALKEEPERS

1091. During the 1966-67 Championship winning season United used 3 goalkeepers in their 42 league games. Name two of them.

1092. At the start of the 1969-70 season who played in goal for the Reds' first 3 league games before losing the No. 1 shirt for most of the remaining season?

1093. Tony Coton played against United at Old Trafford on 7 April 1984. Can you name the team he was playing for?

1094. Who was the Reds' substitute goalkeeper for the 1994 Coca-Cola Cup Final?

1095. Where was Ray Wood born - London, Manchester or Newcastle?

1096. Name the United goalkeeper who enjoyed a Testimonial Dinner in March 1977.

1097. From which Midlands club did United receive Jeff Wealands on-loan from in February 1983?

1098. Who was in goal for the Reds when they played Wimbledon at Old Trafford on 30 April 1990?

1099. When United played Arsenal on 18 October 1975, United's goalkeeper was playing against his former club. Name the goalkeeper concerned.

1100. Can you name the goalkeeper who replaced Alex Stepney in goal for a period during 1975?

RUUD

1101. In what year did Ruud sign for United?

1102. From what club did United purchase Ruud?

1103. Can you recall the Dutch club where Ruud began his football career?

1104. In what year did he make his international debut for Holland - 1997, 1998 or 1999?

1105. What Football Award did Ruud win in 1999?

1106. In what season did he win the Premier League's Golden Boot Award?

1107. Against what neighbouring Country did Ruud make his Holland debut?

1108. How much did United pay for Ruud?

1109. Ruud scored twice in his Premier League debut for United. What London team were on the receiving end of a 3-2 defeat?

1110. What injury delayed Ruud's move to Old Trafford?

TRIVIA - 14

1111. What do Billy the Goat, Major the Saint Bernard and Cyril the Swan all have in common?

1112. True or False, Manchester United inherited their nickname, The Red Devils, from Salford Rugby Club?

1113. Can you name the former Manchester United manager who managed Atletico Madrid in 1989?

1114. How many trophies were United awarded for winning the World Club Championship on 30 November 1999?

1115. Following on from Q1114, how many times in succession had a European team won the trophy following the Reds success?

1116. Can you name the player who was voted as Manchester United's Greatest Player of the 20th Century in a poll conducted by the club's website?

1117. Following on from Q1116, who came second?

1118. True or False, Kevin Moran was shown the red card in the 1985 FA Cup Final?

1119. True or False, Sir Alex Ferguson finished ahead of Bill Shankly and Bob Paisley in Four Four Two magazine's vote for the World's Greatest Ever Manager in a poll conducted in March 2000?

1120. Following on from Q1119, in what position did Sir Matt Busby finish?

SEASON 2002-2003 - 2

1121. What team put United out of the UEFA Champions League?

1122. Name the South Coast club United beat 5-1 in the FA Cup 3rd Round.

1123. Who scored United's goal in the 1-1 draw with Manchester City at Old Trafford?

1124. Name the player who scored a hat-trick for United in their 6-2 mauling of Newcastle United at St James' Park.

1125. How far did United progress in the UEFA Champions League?

1126. Can you recall the London club Ruud scored a hat-trick against in May?

1127. Name the Italian team United met in the Group Stages of the UEFA Champions League.

1128. What London team did United beat 6-0 in the 4th Round of the FA Cup?

1129. What was the score of the Manchester Derby at Maine Road?

1130. Who scored his last ever goal for United on the final day of the season?

THE SCANDINAVIAN LINK

1131. How many league appearances did Peter Schmeichel make for the Reds during the 1994-95 season 32, 37 or 42?

1132. Which player's former clubs include Stokke, EIK-Tonsberg and Lyn Oslo?

1133. After leaving United Jesper Olsen played for two French League sides. Name either of them.

1134. In what competition did Henning Berg score his first goal for the Reds?

1135. Which United manager signed John Sivebaek?

1136. Against which club did Ronny Johnsen score his first goal for United?

1137. Up to the end of the 1996-97 season Ole Gunnar Solskjaer had played 10 times for Norway. How many goals did he score in his first 10 appearances?

1138. True or False, Schmeichel played in all 3 of United's Cup ties during October 1997?

1139. When John Sivebaek left Old Trafford in August 1987 he joined a club that United had played in the 1977-78 European Cup Winners' Cup competition. Name the club.

1140. What West Ham United striker was the first Premier League player to score against Peter Schmeichel during the 1997-98 season?

SEASON 2003-2004 - 2

1141. How many points did United end the season with - 75, 76 or 77?

1142. Name the player who scored both United goals in their FA Cup 3rd Round away win at Aston Villa.

1143. Who scored his first goal for United against Wolves In August?

1144. Name the overseas player who scored for United in their 2-1 away defeat to FC Porto in the UEFA Champions League.

1145. What City did Roy Keane score against in a 4-1 win in September?

1146. Can you name the United player who scored against his former club in a 1-1 draw in February?

1147. What City did United beat 4-2 at Old Trafford in the 5th Round of the FA Cup?

1148. Name the player who scored his first Premiership goal for United v Tottenham Hotspur in a 3-0 home win in March.

1149. Can you recall the United defender who scored the only goal of the game in United's 1-0 win over Leicester City in April?

1150. Who scored his last ever goal for United against Everton on Boxing Day in a 3-2 win?

LEGEND - GEORGE BEST

1151. In what year was George born - 1944, 1945 or 1946?

1152. Where in Northern Ireland was George born?

1153. Against what Midlands club did George make his debut for United?

1154. Can you recall the "Home" Country George made his international debut for Northern Ireland against?

1155. What was the first medal George won at United?

1156. In what sport did George's Mother represent Northern Ireland - Athletics, Hockey or Netball?

1157. In what year was George voted European Footballer of the Year?

1158. What age was George when he played his last game for United?

1159. Apart from the Los Angeles Aztecs, name any 1 of the other 2 North American Soccer League teams George played for.

1160. To the nearest 5, how many caps did George win for Northern Ireland?

GERMAN CONFRONTATIONS

1161. Who were the first German club United played in a competitive European fixture?

1162. What was the aggregate score of the game in Q1161 - 3-2, 4-2 or 5-2?

1163. Can you recall the score of the game when United visited Munich for their 1998-99 UEFA Champions League game versus Bayern Munich?

1164. Who scored for United in the game in Q1163?

1165. What is the name of Bayern Munich's home stadium?

1166. In what year did the stadium in Q1165 stage the Olympic Games?

1167. United met a German side in the 1964-65 Inter-Cities Fairs Cup. Name them.

1168. In the game in Q1163 Bayern Munich had a player who won a World Cup winners' medal with France in 1998. Name him.

1169. Can you name the German defender who United attempted to sign during the summer of 1997?

1170. What was significant about United's first goal in the game in Q1163?

LEGEND - DAVID BECKHAM

1171.   What medal did David win with United in 1992?

1172.   Name the French team David scored against in the Group Stages of the 2001-02 UEFA Champions League.

1173.   Can you recall the London club David visited for a trial when he was wearing his Manchester United kit?

1174.   What Football Award did David win in 1997?

1175.   Name the club David spent a period on loan with in 1995.

1176.   What team did David score against in the 1995-96 UEFA Champions League?

1177.   Who were the opposition when David scored his last European goal for United?

1178.   Against what team did David score against in a 3-1 defeat for United on the opening day of the 1995-96 season?

1179.   David scored United's winner in the 1996 FA Cup Semi-Final. Name United's opponents.

1180.   What Country was David sent off against at the 1998 World Cup Finals?

SEASON 2000 - 2001

1181.   How many points did United end the season with - 80, 85 or 90?

1182.   Name the London club who United beat in the FA Cup 3rd Round.

1183.   Name any 1 of United's 3 Group G opponents in the early stages of the UEFA Champions League.

1184.   Who scored his last Premiership goal for United versus Manchester City in April?

1185.   Name the player who scored in 4 of 7 Premiership games between December and New Years Day.

1186.   What London club did United beat 3-1 at Old Trafford on New Years Day?

1187.   Can you recall United's Spanish opponents in Group A of the UEFA Champions League?

1188.   Who scored a superb free kick to give United victory in the season's first Manchester Derby?

1189.   Can you recall the Italian who scored the winning goal against United in the FA Cup 4th Round at Old Trafford?

1190.   What German team put United out of the UEFA Champions League?

KNIGHT OF 1,000 GAMES

1191. What United were their opponents for Alex Ferguson's first game in charge of United?

1192. Against what London team did United record their first victory under Alex Ferguson?

1193. Name the United defender who scored United's first goal under Alex Ferguson.

1194. Who were United's first European opponents under Alex Ferguson?

1195. What team did United play the most times in Alex Ferguson's 1,000 games as manager?

1196. Name the United player who scored the most number of goals for United in the 1,000 games.

1197. Can you name the London club that United recorded the most number of victories against in the 1,000 games under Alex Ferguson?

1198. What other legendary manager was in charge of United for 1,000 or more games?

1199. Name the United player who made the most appearances for the club in the 1,000 games.

1200. Against what French team was Sir Alex's 1,000th in charge of United?

OWEN HARGREAVES

1201.   In what country was Owen born?

1202.   Can you recall England's South American opponents during the 2006 Fifa World Cup Finals when Owen was booed during the game after coming on as a substitute?

1203.   Can you name Bayern Munich's General Manager and 3-times European Cup winner who said Owen would not be joining Manchester United after the 2006 Fifa World Cup Finals?

1204.   In what year did Owen make his full international debut for England?

1205.   When Owen made his England debut their opponents were the former runners-up in two Fifa World Cup Finals. Name them.

1206.   Against what team did Owen make his Manchester United debut?

1207.   In what year did Owen make his debut for Bayern Munich?

1208.   Name the team Owen played for in Canada.

1209.   What age was Owen when he signed for Manchester United?

1210.   How many euros did Manchester United pay Bayern Munich for Owen's services – 16m, 17m or 18m?

SEASON 1999-2000 - 2

1211. Against what team did the Champions kick-off the defence of their League title?

1212. How many points did the Reds finish the season with 90, 91 or 92?

1213. At what club's ground did United clinch the title?

1214. How many games were left despite the Reds already being crowned Champions?

1215. How many draws and defeats did United accumulate in the FA Premier League during the season?

1216. How many goals did United score in the FA Premier League 95, 96 or 97?

1217. Can you name the team that put United out of the FA Cup?

1218. Name two of the three teams that inflicted a League defeat on the Reds?

1219. Against what club did Ronny Johnsen make his FA Premier League comeback during the season?

1220. Can you name the United striker who considered retiring from International football in March 2000?

THE 1999/2000 FIFA CLUB WORLD CHAMPIONSHIP

1221. Can you name the country where the inaugural FIFA Club World Championship was staged in January 2000?

1222. In which stadium did United play all of their Group games?

1223. Where did United finish in their Group?

1224. Who missed a penalty for the Reds against Ryos del Necaxa?

1225. Who scored for United in their 3-1 loss to Vasco da Gama?

1226. How many United players were sent off in the competition?

1227. Which game did the player above miss as a result of his sending off?

1228. Who scored twice for the Reds against South Melbourne?

1229. Can you name the United player who wore the No.4 shirt during the competition?

1230. Name the team who were crowned FIFA Club World Champions

MIXED BAG - 4

1231.   Name either of Ole Gunnar Solskjaer's two previous clubs.

1232.   What was the first major trophy that United won under the management of Alex Ferguson and in what year was it won?

1233.   Which London club did the Reds defeat in the Semi-Final of the 1983 Milk Cup?

1234.   The father of one of United's 1999 European Cup winning side was a Champion Wrestler. Name the player.

1235.   Against which team did Dwight Yorke score his 20th league goal of the 1999-2000 FA Premier League season?

1236.   What Italian Serie A side did Massimo Taibi go on loan to during the 1999-2000 season?

1237.   What two major Football Awards did Roy Keane win for season 1999-2000?

1238.   True or False, Ryan Giggs made his Manchester United debut against Everton in a Premier League game at Old Trafford on 2 March 1991?

1239.   Can you name the Dutch footballer Manchester United attempted to sign in April 2000 only for the transfer to collapse over a failed medical?

1240.   Name the £15million rated FA Premier League striker who United were linked with only 2 days after the 1999-2000 season had ended.

TRIVIA - 15

1241.　True or False, Sir Alex Ferguson was named FA Carling Premier League Manager of the Year for the sixth time in eight seasons in May 2000?

1242.　Name the former United midfielder who became the first Dutchman to play in an English FA Cup Final.

1243.　Can you name the future Arsenal player who played against United in the 1991 European Super Cup Final?

1244.　Can you name the Portuguese international Manchester United were linked with in May 2000?

1245.　From which French side did the Reds sign Fabien Barthez?

1246.　How much did Fabien Barthez cost United - £7.2m, £7.6m or £7.8m?

1247.　Name the 4 United players who were named in Kevin Keegan's England squad for Euro'2000.

1248.　Can you name the United player who scored his 50th goal for the club against Tottenham Hotspur at Old Trafford on 6 May 2000?

1249.　Name the on-loan United player who scored for Barnsley against Manchester City in a Nationwide Division 1 game on 11 March 2000.

1250.　Four Manchester United players made the PFA Team of the Year for the 1999-2000 season. Can you name three of them?

ANSWERS

LEGEND - ERIC CANTONA 1
1.   The 1992-93 FA Premier League
2.   Leeds United
3.   1996-97
4.   Paris
5.   Manchester City
6.   Auxerre
7.   17
8.   True
9.   The Charity Shield (for Leeds United v Liverpool)
10. A Rugby player

THE BUSBY BABES
11. 1952-1953
12. 5 (1952-1953 to 1956-1957 inclusive)
13. 9th (1957-1958)
14. 3 (1951-1952, 1955-1956 & 1956-1957)
15. Cardiff City (at Old Trafford on 4 April 1953)
16. 1 (2-1 away to Sunderland on 7 April 1958)
17. Newcastle United
18. 11
19. The European Youth Cup
20. 103 (in 42 games)

SEASON 2003 - 2004 - 1
21. Bolton Wanderers
22. Glasgow Rangers, Panathinaikos & VFB Stuttgart
23. 0-0
24. Kleberson
25. Arsenal
26. Southampton
27. Paul Scholes
28. FC Porto (they went on to win it)
29. Wolverhampton Wanderers
30. Liverpool & Blackburn Rovers

LEGEND - OLE GUNNAR SOLSKJAER
31. £1.5million
32. Kristiansund
33. Clausenengen FK & Molde
34. True (versus Blackburn Rovers at Old Trafford on 25 August 1996)
35. Jean-Pierre Papin

36.	18 (19 in all competitions)
37.	SK Rapid Wien (known as Rapid Vienna on 25 September 1996)
38.	Middlesbrough (in the 3-3 draw at Old Trafford on 5 May 1997)
39.	False (he made his FA Cup debut as a substitute for Andy Cole in United's 3rd Round 2-0 win over Spurs at Old Trafford on 5 January 1997. Scholes & Beckham scored.)
40.	Leicester City (at Filbert Street on 3 May 1997)

UNITED MANAGERS

41.	Ernest Mangnall
42.	False (Tommy Docherty was manager)
43.	1977
44.	The FA Cup in 1990
45.	1951-1952
42.	3 (the FA Cup Finals of 1983 & 1985 and the 1983 Milk Cup Final)
47.	12th (season 1928-1929)
48.	Once only (1979-1980)
49.	A. Scott Duncan (Walter Crickmer was the Club Secretary)
50.	Wilf McGuinness

TRIVIA 1

51.	Ian Botham (the England cricketer who had also played football for Scunthorpe United)
52.	The South Atlantic Fund - at the time of The Falkands War
53.	1902
54.	Manchester Central (it was rejected because it was also the name of a local train station)
55.	£350,000
56.	Manchester United Junior Athletic Club
57.	It was their last game at Bank Street before moving to Old Trafford in February 1910.
58.	Billy Meredith (he re-joined Manchester City after spending 15 years with the Reds)
59.	Dixie Dean
60.	115 (a club record)

NEWTON HEATH 1

61.	1878
62.	The Lancashire & Yorkshire Railway
63.	After drawing 2-2 with Fleetwood Rangers on 30 October 1886 the Newton Heath players refused to play extra-time and thus, the game was awarded to their opponents.
64.	1888-1889
65.	The Football Alliance
66.	The Heathens
67.	The Manchester Senior Cup (1892-1893)
68.	North Road, Newton Heath
69.	16th (seasons 1892-1893 & 1893-1894)
70.	The original colours of Green & Gold (Yellow) jerseys & White shorts were replaced by White jerseys & Blue shorts

GUESS MY NAME

71. David Sadler
72. Shay Brennan
73. Bill Foulkes
74. Johnny Carey
75. Nobby Stiles
76. Lee Sharpe
77. Paul Parker
78. Gary Neville
79. John Connelly
80. Harry Gregg

THE 1980's 1

81. Sammy McIlroy (versus Wolverhampton Wanderers on 3 October 1981)
82. 3 (West Ham United - Round 3, Luton Town - Round 4 & Arsenal in the Semi-Final)
83. 4th
84. 1980-1981 (Garry Birtles in October 1980)
85. Michael Knighton (the deal subsequently did not take place)
86. Arsenal (4-2 at home & 2-1 away)
87. Gordon Strachan (3rd Round, 1st leg at Old Trafford on 28.11.82)
88. Arthur Albiston (39) (Gary Bailey 38 & Bryan Robson 32)
89. 1981-1982
90. Luton Town (1-1 at Kennilworth Road on 5 October 1985)

NAME THE TEAM 1

1. Alex Stepney
2. Jimmy Nicholl
3. Arthur Albiston
4. Sammy McIlroy
5. Brian Greenhoff
6. Martin Buchan
7. Steve Coppell
8. Jimmy Greenhoff
9. Stuart Pearson
10. Lou Macari
11. Gordon Hill
Sub. David McCreery

CHAMPIONS 2006-07 – 1

91. Charlton Athletic
92. John O'Shea
93. Marcello Lippi 9Italy's 2006 Fifa World Cup winning coach)
94. He made his 50tth appearance for United
95. Fulham
96. Cristiano Ronaldo (a penalty)
97. 89

98.   Reading

99.   Henrik Larsson

100.   Carlos Tevez (he scored for West Ham United in their 1-0 win over United on the final day of the season)

HISTORY 1

101.   2 (1982 & 1986)

102.   Mark Hughes

103.   He went to Buckingham Palace to receive his Knighthood from the Queen.

104.   3 (1952, 1956 & 1957)

105.   White (United beat Liverpool 2-0)

106.   Children In Need

107.   Denis Law

108.   Gerry Daly

109.   3 (1979, 1983 & 1985)

110.   £15

LEGEND - BRYAN ROBSON

111.   Ron Atkinson

112.   £1.7million

113.   The FA Cup (in 1983)

114.   1993-94

115.   Captain Marvel

116.   Middlesbrough

117.   Terry Venables

118.   90

119.   Bradford City

120.   Gary Megson

FA CUP 1

121.   Mark Hughes

122.   Princess Michael of Kent

123.   Hereford United (United won 1-0)

124.   Exeter City (they share the same name as Newcastle United's ground)

125.   Barnsley

126.   1 (1977)

127.   Norman Whiteside

128.   Cantona, Keane & Kanchelskis

129.   Noel Cantwell (United won 3-1)

130.   Osvaldo Ardiles (Spurs beat United 1-0)

UNITED INTERNATIONALS 1

131.   Stewart Houston (at Hampden Park on 29 October 1975)

132.   Norway (in Bergen on 4 June 1963, Scotland lost 4-2)

133.   They were all substitute appearances

134.   Marco Van Basten (of Holland)

135. His nose (against Southampton at The Dell)
136. None
137. Gordon Strachan
138. Zaire (1974)
139. The European Cup Winners' Cup (v Athletico Madrid in 1991-1992)
140. True (v Yugoslavia at the World Cup in Spain in 1982)

SEASON 2002 - 2003 - 1
141. WBA
142. Ole Gunnar Solskjaer
143. Bolton Wanderers (at Old Trafford)
144. Diego Forlan
145. Newcastle United
146. Sunderland
147. Everton
148. 83
149. Manchester United 4 Real Madrid 3
150. FC Basle

TRIVIA 2
151. It was the first league goal scored by a Manchester United player [after changing the name of the club from Newton Heath]
152. None [he didn't play]
153. 1906-07
154. It was their 1,000th victory in a Division 1 game
155. True
156. 1980
157. 48,388
158. Mark Hughes
159. True [he made 1 appearance as a substitute v Ipswich Town at Old Trafford on 22 August 1992]
160. Steve Bruce

THE 1960's
161. Liverpool [at Anfield]
162. Alex Stepney [35 games] David Gaskell [5 games]
163. West Ham United [3-1 defeat at Hillsborough]
164. 28
165. 1962 [12 July]
166. Bill Foulkes
167. 7th
168. Southampton [3-1 at Villa Park]
169. Shay Brennan & Tony Dunne
170. SL Benfica [Quarter-Final of 1965-66 & Final of 1967-68]

SEASON 1997-1998 : 1

171.   Leeds United [at Elland Road on 27 September 1997]
172.   Bolton Wanderers
173.   West Ham United [at Old Trafford on 13 September 1997]
174.   False [beat Spurs [a], Southampton [h] & drew with Leicester City [a]]
175.   Giggs 2, Scholes & Poborsky
176.   Feyenoord [5/11/97], Arsenal [9/11/97] & Wimbledon [22/11/97]
177.   Nicky Butt [v Tottenham Hotspur on the opening day of the season]
178.   Ramon Vega
179.   Ole Gunnar Solskjaer
180.   David Beckham

LEGEND - ANDY COLE

181. Ipswich Town [at Old Trafford on 4 March 1995]
182.   2
183.   Liverpool's defender Kvarme
184.   17
185.   True
186.   Liverpool's Neil Ruddock
187.   1990
188.   1
189.   Coventry City [at Old Trafford on 30 August 1997]
190.   12 January 1995

LEGENDS 1

191.   1 [the 1968 European Cup]
192.   Bobby Charlton & Denis Law
193.   5
194.   1 [versus Northern Ireland in 1954]
195.   Preston North End
196.   Mark Jones
197.   Le Havre
198.   Lou Macari
199.   Frank O'Farrell
200.   John Gidman [ex-Everton player]

NAME THE TEAM 2

1.   Pat Dunne
2.   Shay Brennan
3.   Tony Dunne
4.   Bill Foulkes
5.   Paddy Crerand
6.   Nobby Stiles
7.   John Connelly
8.   David Herd
9.   Bobby Charlton

10.	Denis Law
11.	George Best

TRIVIA 3

201.	The violin
202.	3 [1982, 1986 & 1990]
203.	The MBE
204.	Bobby Charlton
205.	True
206.	Bill Shankly
207.	Bryan Robson
208.	Brighton & Hove Albion
209.	Jimmy Murphy
210.	None

LEGEND - PAUL INCE

211.	Ilford
212.	West Ham United
213.	1989
214.	The FA Cup (1990)
215.	The Guvnor
216.	Inter Milan
217.	Liverpool
218.	Millwall (United won 5-1)
219.	Wolverhampton Wanderers
220.	Bryan Robson - Middlesbrough

NAME MY FORMER CLUB

221.	Joe Jordan	Leeds United
222.	Gary Pallister	Middlesbrough
223.	Cloin Gibson	Aston Villa
224.	Ian Ure	Arsenal
225.	Dion Dublin	Cambridge United
226.	John Connelly	Burnley
227.	Johnny Carey	St James' Gate
228.	Sandy Turnbull	Manchester City
229.	Ted MacDougall	Bournemouth
230.	Maurice Setters	West Bromwich Albion

LEGEND - DENIS LAW

231.	Torino
232.	1962
233.	£115,000 (a British record transfer fee at the time)
234.	The FA Cup (in 1963)
235.	6
236.	Huddersfield Town

237.   Joe Baker
238.   European Footballer of the Year
239.   Sir Matt Busby, Wilf McGuinness, Frank O'Farrell &Tommy Docherty
240.   Wales (he scored in a 2-1 win in Cardiff in 1958)

THE LEAGUE CUP

241.   Norman Whiteside (Liverpool won 2-1 after extra-time)
242.   Bristol Rovers
243.   Division 2
244.   Blackpool (Blackpool won 5-1 at Bloomfield Road in Round 2)
245.   Mark Bosnich, Paul McGrath & Les Sealey
246.   One (Andrei Kanchelskis in the 1994 Final)
247.   Paddy Roche
248.   Sheffield Wednesday
249.   Gordon McQueen
250.   False (Peter Schmeichel was suspended)

TRIVIA 4

251.   Everton
252.   Roger Byrne
253.   Colombia [in Bogota on 20 May 1970]
254.   Harry Gregg
255.   3
256.   Bill Foulkes
257.   1885
258.   George Best & Bobby Charlton
259.   Wolverhampton Wanderers [1953 & 1954]
260.   None

ALMOST A RED

261.   Glenn Hoddle (Alan Brazil was still at Ipswich Town)
262.   Gerry Francis
263.   David O' Leary
264.   Phil Parkes
265.   Marcello Salas
266.   River Plate
267.   Charlie Nicholas
268.   Nadal
269.   Jim Blyth
270.   Mark Lawrenson (he joined Liverpool)

EUROPEAN CUP WINNERS' CUP

271.   Feyenoord Stadium, Rotterdam (United won the ECWC there in 1991)
272.   Lee Sharpe
273.   Cesar Menoti
274.   PAE Athinaikos (Round 1, 1991-1992)

275. Round 2 (lost to FC Porto)
276. Fourth Division
277. Alan Davies
278. Tottenham Hotspur (2-0 in Round 2, 1st leg at White Hart Lane in 1963-1964 ECWC)
279. Mark Hughes (at Old Trafford on 6 November 1991)
280. Zubizarreta

NANI
281. 1.   £17m
282. Sporting Lisbon
283. Luis Carlos Almeida de Cunha
284. Cape Verde
285. Tottenham Hotspur
286. FC Porto
287. Spartak Moscow
288. Denmark
289. No. 18
290. 20-years old

HISTORY 2
291. The Bells Manager of the Month Award
292. Dave Sexton
293. Eric Cantona
294. Goalkeeper
295. Denis Irwin
296. Stepney, Dawson & Forsyth
297. The O.B.E.
298. Admiral
299. True (versus Sheffield United at Bramall Lane, after only 5 minutes, on the opening day of the 1992-1993 season)
300. Dave Sexton

NAME THE TEAM 3
1. Peter Schmeichel
2. Paul Parker
3. Denis Irwin
4. Steve Bruce
5. Mike Phelan
6. Gary Pallister
7. Andrei Kanchelskis
8. Paul Ince
9. Brian McClair
10. Mark Hughes
11. Ryan Giggs
Sub   Lee Sharpe

LEGEND - STEVE BRUCE

301.   Concussion
302.   Gillingham
303.   He wasn't selected
304.   Captain's Log
305.   1987
306.   Sheffield United
307.   Newcastle
308.   West Ham United (at Old Trafford on 1 September 1993)
309.   He scored United's first goal of the game
310.   Daisy & Dolly

THE 1970's

311.   West Bromwich Albion & Nottingham Forest
312.   Juventus (UEFA Cup, Round 2, 1st leg)
313.   False (Liverpool were)
314.   Hibernian
315.   The Reds Are Back
316.   Steve Coppell & Gordon Hill
317.   Sunderland
318.   Tommy Docherty was sacked
319.   Alan Sunderland
320.   Hooliganism

LEGEND - BOBBY CHARLTON

321.   1954
322.   Charlton Athletic
323.   First Division Championship (1957)
324.   Bill Foulkes
325.   Anglo-Italian Tournament (versus Verona, he scored twice)
326.   Southampton
327.   1958 (versus Scotland at Hampden Park)
328.   Jack Charlton
329.   European Footballer of the Year & The Football Writers' Player of the Year Award
330.   247

SPONSORS & ADVERTISEMENTS

331.   Playtex
332.   Ford (a Ford Cortina)
333.   Adidas
334.   Sharp UK Limited
335.   White
336.   Birthdays (part of the Football Souvenir Company)
337.   Norman Whiteside
338.   Adidas
339.   Pony

340.   Guinness

FIND THE PLAYER
341.   Russell Beardsmore
342.   Mike Phelan
343.   Danny Wallace
344.   Harry Gregg
345.   John Connelly
346.   Warren Bradley
347.   Noel Cantwell
348.   Roger Byrne
349.   Carlo Satori
350.   David Gaskell

TRIVIA 5
351.   One (Gordon Strachan)
352.   Ken Doherty (1997 World Professional Snooker Champion)
353.   Eric Harrison
354.   Third (1. Duncan Edwards 2. Jimmy Greaves)
355.   Ultimate United
356.   Gary Bailey
357.   Dublin (9th July 1951)
358.   2 (1977 & 1979)
359.   1967 (season 1966-1967)
360.   Sing Up For The Champions

FA CUP FINALS
361.   Blue
362.   2 (1957 & 1958)
363.   £2.50
364.   He had been sent off during the game (he received his medal after an appeal to the
        Football Association)
365.   Stewart Houston
366.   McGrath, Moran, Stapleton & Whiteside
367.   One (1963)
368.   Jimmy Greenhoff
369.   Jack Rowley
370.   Jim McCalliog (his pass to Bobby Stokes led to Southampton's goal)

AN EARLY BATH
371.   Mark Hughes   1992 v Moscow Torpedo (UEFA Cup)
372.   Eric Cantona   1994 v Glasgow Rangers (Friendly)
373.   Roy Keane   1995 v Blackburn R. (Premier League)
374.   Nicky Butt   1996 v West Ham Utd (Premier League)
375.   Eric Cantona   1994 v Arsenal (Premier League)
376.   Pat McGibbon   1995 v York City (League Cup)

377.	Peter Schmeichel	1994 v Charlton Athletic (FA Cup)
378.	Andrei Kanchelskis	1994 v Aston Villa (League Cup Final)
379.	Eric Cantona	1993 v Galatasaray (European Cup)
380.	Roy Keane	1995 v Middlesbrough (Premier League)

SPOT THE PLAYER

381.	William Wrigglesworth	Forward 1936 - 1947
382.	Jeff Whitefoot	Half-Back 1949 - 1956
383.	Henry Cockburn	Half-Back 1946 - 1955
384.	Wilson Greenwood	Forward 1900 - 1901
385.	Horace Blew	Full-Back 1905 - 1906
386.	Alan Foggon	Forward 1976 - 1977
387.	Arnold Sidebottom	Half-Back 1972 - 1975
388.	Stanley Gallimore	Forward 1903 - 1904
389.	Albert Quixall	Forward 1958 - 1964
390.	John Moody	Goalkeeper 1931 - 1933

CHARITY SHIELD

391.	Frank Sinclair (De Matteo put his penalty over the crossbar)
392.	Nicky Butt
393.	Queens Park Rangers
394.	17
395.	1990 (1 -1 with Liverpool)
396.	Tottenham Hotspur (1967)
397.	True (versus Swindon Town in 1911)
398.	Harlod Halse with 6 goals (Charlton 2 & Meredith 1)
399.	1985 (versus Everton)
400.	4

NAME THE TEAM 4

1	Gary Bailey
2.	Mike Duxbury
3.	Arthur Albiston
4.	Ray Wilkins
5.	Kevin Moran
6.	Gordon McQueen
7.	Bryan Robson
8.	Arnold Muhren
9.	Frank Stapleton
10.	Norman Whiteside
11.	Alan Davies

THE CAPTAIN'S ARMBAND

401.	Martin Buchan
402.	George Graham
403.	Mike Phelan

404. Pat Crerand
405. Ray Wood
406. Ray Wilkins
407. Bryan Robson
408. Noel Cantwell
409. Steve Bruce
410. Frank Stapleton

LEGENDS 2

411. Arsenal (United won 3-1)
412. Jimmy Greenhoff
413. Laurie Cunningham
414. Norman Whiteside
415. Jimmy Rimmer (with Aston Villa)
416. Devon
417. Alan Davies
418. He opened a pet shop
419. False
420. Coventry City (United won 4-1)

THE MANAGEMENT GAME

421. £200,000
422. Lou Macari & Stuart Pearson
423. Rochdale
424. Coventry City
425. Chelsea
426. Wolverhampton Wanderers
427. Ron Atkinson (Cambridge United won Division 4)
428. Tommy Docherty & Alex Ferguson
429. West Bromwich Albion
430. Tommy Docherty (Denis joined Manchester City)

MIXED BAG 1

431. 1983-1984 (16 goals)
432. A Question Of Sport
433. Galatasaray (European Cup tie at Old Trafford)
434. George Best
435. Billy McNeill
436. The Festival Of Britain
437. Manchester City
438. Surprise Surprise
439. 2nd
440. Pentonville

ENGLAND UNITED

441. Roger Byrne & Bill Foulkes

442.	Bryan Robson
443.	Ray Wilkins
444.	1985 (versus Republic of Ireland at Wembley, England won 2-1)
445.	Leeds United
446.	Bryan Robson (The Bryan Robson Scanner Appeal)
447.	Neil Webb (Paul Ince was No.2)
448.	Stuart Pearson (England won 1-0 on 8 May)
449.	False (he won his only England cap in 1977 when he was at Aston Villa)
450.	1976 (versus Italy on 28 May, England won 3-2)

TRIVIA 6

451.	True
452.	Chelsea (FA Cup, 3rd Round at Stamford Bridge on 4 January)
453.	One (1977 versus Liverpool, Score 0-0)
454.	6-2
455.	Nikola Jovanovic (United won 5-0)
456.	Dave Sexton (he arrived in January 1978 on trial)
457.	Dennis Viollet (4) & Tommy Taylor (3)
458.	None (he was a Squad member only)
459.	Jimmy Rimmer
460.	1984 (May)

MOVING ON 1

461.	Andrei Kanchelskis	Everton
462.	Gary Walsh	Middlesbrough
463.	Mike Phelan	West Bromwich Albion
464.	Colin McKee	Kilmarnock
465.	Mark Robins	Norwich City
466.	Keith Gillespie	Newcastle United
467.	Mal Donaghy	Chelsea
468.	Viv Anderson	Sheffield Wednesday
469.	Jim Leighton	Dundee
470.	Colin Gibson	Leicester City

SEASON 1997-1998 : 2

471.	Arsenal (0-1 at Old Trafford on 14 March 1998)
472.	Blackburn Rovers (3-1)
473.	Newcastle United (1-1 at Old Trafford on 18 April 1998)
474.	AS Monaco (France)
475.	Crystal Palace & Leeds United
476.	Wesley Brown
477.	Barnsley (a)
478.	2-0 Andy Cole & Teddy Sheringham
479.	Danny Higginbotham
480.	One - United finished on 77 points.

NAME A TEAM

481. Athletico Madrid, Athletic Bilbao, AZ Alkmaar, Ajax Amsterdam & Austria Wien
482. True
483. Dukla Prague
484. Ferencvaros (1-2 (a) in the Semi-Final Play-Off game)
485. Glentoran
486. Hannover 1896
487. Maccabi Haifa
488. True
489. FK Partizan Belgrade (1965-66 Semi-Final, United lost 1-2 on agg.)
490. Athletic Bilbao (Quarter-Final) & Real Madrid (Semi-Final)

THE BOSS

491. The European Cup Winners' Cup & The European Super Cup
492. Dunfermline Athletic
493. £55,000
494. He became Scotland's most expensive footballer
495. Queensland Star
496. It is named after a ship (which his father helped to build)
497. East Stirlingshire
498. 7
499. None
500. 1

NAME THE TEAM 5

1. Alex Stepney
2. Shay Brennan
3. Tony Dunne
4. Paddy Crerand
5. Bill Foulkes
6. Nobby Stiles
7. George Best
8. Brian Kidd
9. Bobby Charlton
10. David Sadler
11. John Aston

NAME THE YEAR 1

501. 1988
502. 1991
503. 1974
504. 1978
505. 1994
506. 1968
507. 1958

508.	1980
509.	1963
510.	1981

SEASON 1998-1999 1

511.	Sheffield Wednesday (United won 3-0 on 17 April 1999)
512.	18
513.	Leeds United (Cole scored at Elland Road in a 1-1 draw)
514.	Gary Walsh
515.	Newcastle United (0-0 on 8 November 1998)
516.	Sheffield Wednesday (he came on for Jaap Stam)
517.	3 (Arsenal (a) 0-3, Sheffield Wednesday (a) 1-3 & Middlesbrough (h) 2-3)
518.	Ronny Johnsen (Nicky Butt then replaced him)
519.	Charlton Athletic (at The Valley on 31 January)
520.	80

CUP COMPETITIONS

521.	Wolverhampton Wanderers [0-1 away in the 3rd Round]
522.	FA Youth Cup Final [1-1 [a] & 4-1 [h]]
523.	Waterford
524.	Ajax Amsterdam [Round 1, United won 2-1 on aggregate]
525.	Atletico Madrid [a] [Round 2, 1st leg]
526.	1 [season 1982-1983]
527.	Manchester City [Maine Road]
528.	1 [0-1 away to Gornik Zagreb in the Quarter-Final, 2nd leg]
529.	Norwich City [1-2 away in the 5th Round]
530.	Ryan Giggs

ALL MIXED UP

531.	Remi Moses
532.	1984-1985 [Round 1]
533.	True [Celtic lost 1-4]
534.	Walter Winterbottom
535.	Paul Scholes [v Italy in Le Tournoi De France on 4 June 1997]
536.	Celta Vigo
537.	6th
538.	Jimmy Murphy [United's Assistant Manager under Sir Matt Busby]
539.	Steve McClaren [as Assistant Manager from Derby County]
540.	Andy Cole

LEGENDS 3

541.	True (19 December 1972)
542.	Arsenal
543.	Maurice Setters
544.	205
545.	£18,000

156

546.   Ruud Gullit (later managed Chelsea & Newcastle United)
547.   Arsenal
548.   Harry Gregg
549.   Oldham Athletic
550.   £300,000

UNITED IN PRINT

551.   George Best   Best Of Both Worlds
552.   Noel Cantwell   United We Stand
553.   Alex Stepney   In Safe Keeping
554.   Lou Macari   United - We Shall Not Be Moved
555.   Denis Law   Living For Kicks
556.   Harry Gregg   Wild About Football
557.   Tommy Docherty   Call The Doc
558.   Alan Gowling   Football Inside Out
559.   Gary & Philip Neville   For Club And Country
560.   Jimmy Murphy   Matt, United And Me

LEGEND - PADDY CRERAND

561.   Glasgow Celtic
562.   1963 (February)
563.   1961 (versus the Republic of Ireland)
564.   16
565.   304
566. · Blackpool
567.   FK Partizan Belgrade
568.   FA Cup (1963)
569.   Tommy Docherty
570.   Northampton Town

1998-1999 PRE-SEASON

571.   Huddersfield Town
572.   Jack Rowley
573.   Kevin Pilkington
574.   Motherwell
575.   Andy Cole
576.   Ryan Giggs' goal versus Juventus
577.   Patrick Kluivert
578.   FC Barcelona
579.   Sheffield United
580.   Steve Bruce

MUNICH MEMORIAL GAME

581.   457 days [versus West Ham United on 11th May 1997]
582.   Roy Keane
583.   Eric Cantona European XI

584.   2-2
585.   Martin Dahlin
586.   Mark Wilson
587.   4 - Eric Cantona, Mark Hughes, William Prunier & Bryan Robson
588.   Laurent Blanc
589.   Pascal Olmeta
590.   Manchester United 8 Eric Cantona European XI 4

TRIVIA 7

591.   Harry Gregg
592.   Hidetoshi Nakata
593.   Perugia [Italy]
594.   Andy Cole
595.   Arsenal [Tottenham Hotspur were the opponents]
596.   Crystal Palace
597.   Paul Ince
598.   Borussia Dortmund [1997 European Cup winners]
599.   Tottenham Hotspur
600.   £575million

NAME THE TEAM 6

1.   Peter Schmeichel
2.   Paul Parker
3.   Denis Irwin
4.   Steve Bruce
5.   Andrei Kanchelskis
6.   Gary Pallister
7.   Eric Cantona
8.   Paul Ince
9.   Roy Keane
10.   Mark Hughes
11.   Ryan Giggs
Subs   Lee Sharpe & Brian McClair

SEASON 1999 - 2000 - 1

601.   Dwight Yorke
602.   Sheffield Wednesday
603.   None (they opted out of it to play in a FIFA Tournament in Brazil)
604.   Andy Cole
605.   28
606.   Chelsea
607.   Fiorentina
608.   West Ham United
609.   Jordi Cruyff
610.   David Beckham (versus Real Madrid)

HISTORY 3

611.   True (because of the damage to Old Trafford United had to play their home games at Maine Road)
612.   A goat
613.   Aston Villa
614.   Harry Gregg
615.   Bill Foulkes
616.   The Outcasts
617.   For the right to form a Players' Union
618.   Dennis Viollet [United won 3-1 at Old Trafford on 4 January 1958]
619.   False [the jersey was red & white vertical stripes]
620.   John Robson

TRIVIA 8

621.   Luton Town [season 1960-1961]
622.   False
623.   Eyal Berkovic
624.   Leicester City
625.   Henning Berg
626.   Wimbledon [28 March 1998]
627.   Bayern Munich [UEFA Champions League, 30 September 1998]
628.   1 [Arsenal 78pts, United 77pts]
629.   None, the smallest was 55,008 v Southampton on 13 August 1997
630.   Lothar Mathaus

SEASON 1998-1999 2

631.   Leicester City
632.   2-2
633.   Teddy Sheringham
634.   Charlton Athletic [Old Trafford on 9 September]
635.   Arsenal [away to Arsenal on 20 September]
636.   Arsenal 3 Manchester United 0
637.   Southampton [at the Dell on 3 October]
638.   A stomach strain
639.   West Ham United [at Upton Park on 22 August]
640.   Charlton Athletic [9 September]

SCOTLAND UNITED

641.   30
642.   Timothy
643.   Preston North End & Chelsea
644.   34 [in 44 appearances]
645.   Brian McClair
646.   Jim Holton
647.   Mexico 1986
648.   Martin Buchan

649.   5
650.   1983

TRIVIA 9

651.   7 [season 1961-1962]
652.   Dundee
653.   Malaysia
654.   Dynamo Kiev
655.   Gary Bailey
656.   £40,000
657.   1987
658.   Brian with 267 appearances [Jimmy played 118 games]
659.   2 [1987 & 1989]
660.   False [Paul McGrath & Kevin Moran were the centre-halves]

WALES UNITED

661.   2 [Burnley - League Cup & Aston Villa - League]
662.   Ronald Wyn Davies
663.   2 [Pecsi Munkas (h) & Montpellier (a)]
664.   1991
665.   True
666.   Newcastle United
667.   Southampton
668.   LKS Lodz [UEFA Champions League Qualifier on 12 August]
669.   1958 [Matt Busby was still recovering from the injuries he sustained in the Munich Air Disaster]
670.   2 [1904 with Manchester City & 1909 with United]

IRELAND UNITED

671.   1 [1966-1967]
672.   Norman Whiteside
673.   Frank Stapleton
674.   1963 FA Cup
675.   Cookstown sausages
676.   Dublin
677.   Brentford
678.   Derek Brazil
679.   No's 7 & 11
680.   Birmingham City

FA CUP 2

681.   False [they met Blackburn Rovers who they beat 6-1 (h)]
682.   Sheffield Wednesday [United lost 0-1 at Hillsborough in the 1st Round]
683.   6-4
684.   Shay Brennan
685.   He scored twice in United's 3-0 win over Sheffield Wednesday

686. 1948 [the 1909 Final was played at the Crystal Palace]
687. Tottenham Hotspur [3rd Round]
688. United had a replica of the Cup made and because it had lost its' originality the FA decided to make a new Cup for the following year's competition
689. Brighton & Hove Albion [United beat them in the 1983 Final Replay]
690. AFC Bournemouth

GUESS MY NAME 2

691. Neil Webb
692. Denis Law
693. Eddie Colman
694. Gordon McQueen
695. Steve Coppell
696. Chris Turner
697. Pat Crerand
698. Dion Dublin
699. Gary Pallister
700. Eric Cantona

NAME THE TEAM 7

1. Les Sealey
2. Paul Ince
3. Lee Martin
4. Steve Bruce
5. Mike Phelan
6. Gary Pallister
7. Bryan Robson
8. Neil Webb
9. Brian McClair
10. Mark Hughes
11. Danny Wallace

NUMBER 1 HITS

701. World Club Championship Runners Up — Those Were The Days by Mary Hopkin
702. United are relegated to To Division 2 — Seasons In The Sun by Terry Jacks
703. Eric Cantona's debut — I Will Always Love You by Whitney Houston
704. Premier League Champions — Five Live EP by George Michael & Queen with Lisa Stansfield
705. Alex Ferguson takes charge — Don't Leave Me This Way by The Communards
706. European Cup Winners' Cup Winners — Shoop Shoop Song by Cher

707.	European Super Cup		Dizzy
			By Vic Reeves & The Wonder Stuff
709.	FA Cup Winners		I Don't Wanna Talk About It
			by Rod Stewart
710.	European Cup Winners		Young Girl
			by Union Gap featuring
			Gary Puckett

TRANSFER PRICES

711.	Ted MacDougall	to West Ham United	£170,000
712.	Carlo Satori	to Bologna	£45,000
713.	Ray O'Brien	to Notts County	£40,000
714.	Brian Kidd	to Arsenal	£110,000
715.	Jim McCalliog	to Southampton	£40,000
716.	Jim Holton	to Sunderland	£64,000
717.	Gerry Daly	to Derby County	£175,000
718.	Gordon Hill	to Derby County	£250,000
719.	Jonathan Clark	to Derby County	£50,000
720.	Stuart Pearson	to West Ham United	£220,000

NEWTON HEATH 2

721. They all played for Manchester United as well as Newton Heath
722. Dundee
723. Chesterfield [Newton Heath won 2-0]
724. Division 2
725. 1901-1902
726. 15th
727. False [1894-95, 1895-96, 1896-97, 1897-98 & 1898-99]
728. A. H. Albut
729. Lincoln City [Newton Heath lost 1-2 [h] on 1 December 1901]
730. True

TRIVIA 10

731. True
732. None
733. Gabriel Batistuta & Ariel Ortega
734. 24
735. PFA Young Player Of The Year
736. George Best
737. Neil Webb [he came on as a substitute]
738. None, he didn't play in the Final
739. True [he came on as a substitute for Lee Martin]
740. Pat Crerand

UNITED AT THE WORLD CUP FINALS 1

741. Gary Bailey, Bryan Robson & Ray Wilkins

742. 3
743. John Aston Snr. [Brazil 1950]
744. Paul Parker [then of Queens Park Rangers]
745. Jim Holton [Scotland]
746. 1974 in West Germany
747. Steve Coppell
748. 2 [Harry Gregg of Northern Ireland & Colin Webster of Wales]
749. Martin Buchan [3 games]
750. Bobby Charlton, Alex Stepney & Nobby Stiles

LEGENDS 4
751. Mark Hughes [v Spurs at Old Trafford on 2 May 1992]
752. Brisbane Lions
753. Ian Storey-Moore [from Nottingham Forest in March 1972]
754. Queens Park Rangers
755. Bradford City
756. Jimmy Greenhoff
757. Mark Hughes [v Sheffield United away on 15th August 1992]
758. Coventry, Leicester, Birmingham & Stoke
759. Partick Thistle
760. Stuart Pearson [2], Lou Macari & Jimmy Greenhoff

LEGEND - WILF McGUINNESS
761. 1953
762. Wolverhampton Wanderers
763. 1969 (June)
764. Sir Matt Busby
765. The First Division Championship (1955-56)
766. He broke his leg (in a Central League game v Stoke City)
767. England Youth Team
768. Aris Solonica & Panachaki Patras
769. York City
770. 85

MIXED BAG 2
771. Leeds United
772. Johann Cruyff
773. Archie Knox [he was assistant manager to Alex Ferguson]
774. Andy Ritchie
775. Blackburn Rovers
776. Brian McClair
777. Keith Gillespie [signed from Newcastle United]
778. 2 [1982 & 1986]
779. None [UEFA banned sponsorship on shirts for the competition]
780. £55,000 [from Chelsea]

RE-ARRANGE THE TEAM
781. Raba Vasas ETO
782. Red Star Belgrade
783. Gornik Zagreb
784. Grantham Town
785. New York Select
786. Bradford Park Avenue
787. Stuttgart Kickers
788. Hannover 1896
789. Rotor Volgograd
790. Tevere Roma

TRIVIA 11
791. Jack Crompton
792. Jock Stein
793. True [Walter Crickmer, the Club Secretary, picked the team]
794. Bill Foulkes
795. Mick Quinn [Coventry City]
796. He withdrew players from an England Under-18 game.
797. Decimilisation took place in 1970
798. Dave Sexton
799. Arsenal [away on 20 September 1998]
800. Jordi Cruyff

NAME THE TEAM 8
1. Peter Schmeichel
2. Denis Irwin
3. Lee Martin
4. Steve Bruce
5. Neil Webb
6. Gary Pallister
7. Andrei Kanchelskis
8. Paul Ince
9. Brian McClair
10. Mark Hughes
11. Clayton Blackmore
Sub Ryan Giggs

DEBUTS 1
801. George Graham   Arsenal
802. Harry Gregg   Leicester City
803. Dion Dublin   Southampton
804. Brian Kidd   Everton
805. Billy Meredith   Aston Villa
806. David Sadler   Sheffield Wednesday
807. Denis law   West Bromwich Albion

164

808.	Martin Buchan	Tottenham Hotspur
809.	Wilf McGuinness	Wolverhampton Wanderers
810.	Remi Moses	Middlesbrough

THE 1970's 2

811. Mick Martin & Gerry Daly
812. 5 [Wilf McGuinness, Sir Matt Busby, Frank O'Farrell, Tommy Docherty & Dave Sexton]
813. Burnley [£200,000]
814. Aston Villa [1-1 home] & [1-2 away]
815. 1976-1977 [UEFA Cup]
816. Dave Sexton [Tommy Docherty was sacked in July 1977]
817. Brian Kidd
818. 1970 [after a Second Replay]
819. Ian Storey-Moore
820. 1 [1977, drew 0-0 with Liverpool the League Champions]

SEASON 1998-1999 3

821. There was a power failure in the Trafford Area which caused all of the lighting in the stadium, including the floodlights, to go out.
822. Cole [Andy of Manchester United & Joe of West Ham United]
823. Nick Culkin [Van Der Gouw was in goal whilst Peter Schmeichel was in Barbados on holiday]
824. Bryan Robson, Viv Anderson & Gordon McQueen
825. Brian Kidd [Blackburn Rovers]
826. Everton [Premier League game at Goodison Park on 31 October]
827. 5th Round [Quarter-Final]
828. Tottenham Hotspur [1-3 at White Hart Lane on 2 December]
829. Ryan Giggs
830. Aberdeen [Teddy Scott Testimonial at Pittodrie]

UEFA CHAMPIONS LEAGUE 1998-1999

831. LKS Lodz
832. Bayern Munich, FC Barcelona & IF Brondby
833. Group D
834. Giovane Elber
835. Nicky Butt
836. FC Barcelona, 3-3
837. Bayern Munich [30 September 1998]
838. 1-1
839. 10
840. 20

WINNERS

841.	FA Cup	1909
842.	FA Charity Shield	1993

165

843.	FA Youth Cup	1964
844.	Lancashire FA Youth Cup	1991
845.	Football League Division 1	1952
846.	Central League	1960
847.	Lancashire FA Senior Cup	1969
848.	Manchester FA Senior Cup	1955
849.	Football League Cup	1992
850.	Football League Division 2	1936

TAKE IT AS WORN

851. 1982
852. It had a photograph of Old Trafford printed on it.
853. Green [as were his shirt & shorts]
854. Blue & White vertical stripes
855. The names of past and present Manchester United players.
856. White
857. A Red Rose
858. False
859. White Shirt, Black Shorts [White Socks]
860. United wore Blue Shirts and Blackpool wore White Shirts [both clubs changed from their traditional colours of Red Shirts and Tangerine Shirts respectively]

BIG RON

861. 1981 [June]
862. Frederick
863. Kettering Town
864. Jack Crompton & Harry Gregg
865. Dave Sexton
866. Mick Brown
867. Frank Stapleton
868. Lou Macari [1-2 loss at Coventry City on the opening day of the 1981-1982 season. Ironically Coventry City were managed by Dave Sexton]
869. 1983 FA Cup [4-0 Replay win over Brighton & Hove Albion]
870. Big Ron : A Different Ball Game

UNITED INTERNATIONALS 2

871.	Johnny Berry	Argentina
872.	Bill Foulkes	Northern Ireland
873.	David Pegg	Eire
874.	Nobby Stiles	Scotland
875.	Alex Stepney	Sweden
876.	Jim Holton	England
877.	George Best	Wales
878.	Jimmy Nicholl	Israel
879.	Paddy Roche	USSR
880.	Ashley Grimes	Turkey

FA CUP 3

881. Arthur Albiston
882. 17
883. Middlesbrough [United won 3-1 at Old Trafford]
884. Burnley [United lost 1-2 away]
885. Stan Pearson [8 goals]
886. Andrei Kanchelskis & Brian McClair
887. Andy Cole [away to Barnsley, 2-3 defeat in 5th Round Replay]
888. Chelsea [United won 2-0 at home in the 4th Round] & Arsenal   [United lost 1-2 away in the 5th Round]
889. Danny Wallace
890. Lee Sharpe [for Denis Irwin] & Brian McClair [for Andrei Kanchelskis]

SIR MATT BUSBY

891. General Manager
892. 1945
893. False [he played for Manchester City]
894. Jimmy Murphy
895. Denis Law
896. £8,000
897. 1967
898. 1994 [20th January]
899. 5
900. Glasgow Celtic

NAME THE TEAM 9

1. Gary Bailey
2. John Gidman
3. Arthur Albiston
4. Norman Whiteside
5. Paul McGrath
6. Kevin Moran
7. Bryan Robson
8. Gordon Strachan
9. Frank Stapleton
10. Mark Hughes
11. Jesper Olsen
Sub   Mike Duxbury

FA CARLING PREMIER LEAGUE FIRSTS

901. The first team to beat United.   Sheffield United
902. The first team United drew with.   Ipswich Town
903. The first team United scored against.   Sheffield United
904. The first team to score against United at Old Trafford.   Everton
905. The first team United beat.   Southampton
906. The first team United beat at Old Trafford.   Crystal Palace

907.	The first team United beat away.	Southampton
908.	The first team United scored against at Old Trafford.	Ipswich Town
909.	The first team United beat twice.	Nottingham Forest
910.	The first team to beat United twice.	Chelsea

DEBUTS 2

911.	Ray Wood	Newcastle United
912.	Gordon McQueen	Liverpool
913.	Denis Irwin	Coventry City
914.	Mickey Thomas	Chelsea
915.	Ben Thornley	West Ham United
916.	Bryan Robson	Tottenham Hotspur
917.	Nicky Butt	Oldham Athletic
918.	Jimmy Delaney	Grimsby Town
919.	Alex Stepney	Manchester City
920.	Jimmy Greenhoff	Leicester City

LEADING GOALSCORERS

921.	George Best	1967-1968
922.	Bobby Charlton	1958-1959
923.	David Herd	1961-1962
924.	Gordon Hill	1977-1978
925.	Mark Hughes	1984-1985
926.	Joe Jordan	1979-1980
927.	Denis Law	1962-1963
928.	Lou Macari	1975-1976
929.	Frank Stapleton	1983-1984
930.	Dennis Viollet	1959-1960

THE OPPOSITION

931.	Martin Peters [Spurs won 4-1, Charlton scored for United]
932.	Videoton [Quarter-Final, 2nd leg, United lost 4-5 on penalties]
933.	7 [3 League Cup, 2 FA Cup, 2 Division 1]
934.	Huddersfield Town
935.	Chelsea [a] [FA Cup Quarter-Final, United won 2-0]
936.	RC Strasbourg [Quarter-Final]
937.	AC Milan [Semi-Final, 1957-1958]
938.	West Ham United [League Cup 3rd Round &7 FA Cup 5th Round]
939.	Sporting Lisbon [United won 4-1]
940.	Tottenham Hotspur [1963-1964 ECWC]

UNITED DEFENDERS

941.	The European Cup Winners' Cup [1991]
942.	John Gidman [1985]
943.	Left-back
944.	1988 [versus Hungary when he was with Middlesbrough]

945.   Paul McGrath
946.   Steve Bruce [he was never capped by England]
947.   Stewart Houston
948.   Gary Pallister
949.   David May
950.   Kevin Moran

UNITED FRONTMEN
951.   David Herd
952.   2 [with United in 1977 and with West Ham United in 1980]
953.   Paco Rabane
954.   Republic of Ireland
955.   Teddy Sheringham [then of Tottenham Hotspur]
956.   Brian McClair
957.   Romania
958.   One of the corner flags
959.   A header
960.   Ryan Giggs & Paul Scholes

THE 1980's 2
961.   The Screen Sports Super Cup
962.   1985-1986
963.   Osvaldo Ardiles [of Tottenham Hotspur]
964.   Frank Worthington
965.   Remi Moses
966.   3rd [1981-1982]
967.   Nottingham Forest [19th January 1983]
968.   Arsenal
969.   Villa Park [home of Aston Villa]
970.   Brian McClair [Robson & Bruce were the other scorers]

TRIVIA 12
971.   Terry Cooke
972.   Derby County [United won 1-0 at Old Trafford]
973.   Ron Atkinson
974.   Leicester City [FA Premier League]
975.   Leicester City 2 Manchester United 6
976.   Jaap Stam
977.   Roy Keane
978.   David Beckham
979.   Jim Ryan [Alex Ferguson was attending a family funeral]
980.   False [Manchester City finished the season as Runners-Up]

LEGEND - PETER SCHMEICHEL
981.   £500,000
982.   European Goalkeeper Of The Year

983.   1996
984.   1995-1996 [UEFA Cup versus Rotor Volgograd]
985.   True
986.   Les Sealey
987.   1993
988.   Antonio Conte
989.   Alex Stepney
990.   Bayern Munich [UEFA Champions League Final in Barcelona on 26th May 1999]

NAME THE TEAM 10
1.   Les Sealey
2.   Denis Irwin
3.   Clayton Blackmore
4.   Steve Bruce
5.   Mike Phelan
6.   Gary Pallister
7.   Bryan Robson
8.   Paul Ince
9.   Brian McClair
10.   Mark Hughes
11.   Lee Sharpe

MIXED BAG 3
991.   Walter Smith [of Everton]
992.   York City
993.   Paul Scholes [the game ended 1-1]
994.   Phil Neville
995.   Swedish [his father is Yugoslavian]
996.   Mark Robins
997.   5 [Terry Venables, Glenn Hoddle, Howard Wilkinson, Kevin Keegan & Sven Goran Erikkson]
998.   Paul Scholes
999.   Norwich City
1000.   David Beckham, Nicky Butt, Dion Dublin & Karel Poborsky

TRIVIA 13
1001.   USA (1959), Luxembourg (1960), Mexico (1961) & Switzerland (1963)
1002.   Jaap Stam
1003.   Andrei Kanchelskis (in United's 5-0 win over Manchester City)
1004.   David Beckham, Roy Keane & Dwight Yorke
1005.   33
1006.   Bill Foulkes (Gerd Muller represented Bayern Munich)
1007.   Tottenham Hotspur (United lost 1-3 in the Worthington Cup on 2 December 1998)
1008.   LKS Lodz (a) (2nd Qualifying Round, 26 August 1998)
1009.   FA Cup 34 goals (European competitions 28 goals, League Cup 3 goals)
1010.   Gary Neville (v Spurs at White Hart Lane in a 2-2 draw)

LEGENDS 5

1011.   Remi Moses
1012.   Dave Sexton
1013.   Mike Duxbury
1014.   Alex Stepney
1015.   Jimmy Rimmer [Aston Villa - replaced by Nigel Spink]
1016.   Republic of Ireland 29   Northern Ireland 7
1017.   Allenby Chilton
1018.   Reg Allen [£11,000 from Queens Park Rangers in 1950]
1019.   Frank Stapleton
1020.   Colin Webster

OLD TRAFFORD

1021.   Huddersfield Town and Sheffield Wednesday
1022.   76, 892
1023.   Wolverhampton Wanderers and Grimsby Town
1024.   Ireland
1025.   The World Club Championship game between Manchester United and Estudiantes De Plata (Argentina). The game ended 1-1.
1026.   New Zealand All Blacks (in a Rugby Union game)
1027.   March 1941 (11 March 1941)
1028.   Nottingham Forest (1-1 draw on 22 February 1958)
1029.   The Khaki Cup Final (because of the large number of soldiers in the crowd)
1030.   1910 (19 February 1910)

STRIKE FORCE

1031.   It was his first for United.
1032.   14 (he came on as a substitute for Denis Irwin against Everton at Old Trafford on 2 March 1991)
1033.   5' 4"
1034.   Jesper Olsen
1035.   Jack Rowley
1036.   Stoke City
1037.   Kevin Davies
1038.   1983
1039.   Lou Macari
1040.   9

UNITED v CITY

1041.   1960-1961 & 1961-1962
1042.   True
1043.   None
1044.   1954-1955
1045.   235.   United 0   City 5
1046.   1986
1047.   True

1048.   Francis Lee
1049.   Denis Law
1050.   Arthur Albiston

LEGEND - ERIC CANTONA 2

1051.   Blackburn Rovers [1994 FA Charity Shield]
1052.   False [Steve Bruce captained the side]
1053.   He was dismissed after the game had ended
1054.   A Boxing Promoter
1055.   Prince Albert of Monaco's Select Side
1056.   5
1057.   Auxerre & Olympique Marseille
1058.   Henri Michel
1059.   9 [from 21 appearances in season 1992-1993]
1060.   Blackburn Rovers [United were trying to sign Alan Shearer at the time]

MOVING ON 2

1061.   Harry Gregg   Stoke City
1062.   Lee Sharpe   Leeds United
1063.   David Sadler   Miami Tornados
1064.   Norman Whiteside   Everton
1065.   Chris Turner   Sheffield Wednesday
1066.   Frank Stapleton   Ajax Amsterdam
1067.   Dion Dublin   Coventry City
1068.   Jimmy Greenhoff   Crewe Alexandria
1069.   Lee Martin   Glasgow Celtic
1070.   Mickey Thomas   Everton

WHERE WAS I BORN ?

1071.   Denis Law   Aberdeen
1072.   Steve Bruce   Corbridge
1073.   Bobby Charlton   Ashington
1074.   Stuart Pearson   Hull
1075.   Viv Anderson   Nottingham
1076.   Clayton Blackmore   Neath
1077.   Paul Parker   West Ham
1078.   Shay Brennan   Manchester
1079.   Ian Ure   Ayr
1080.   Roy Keane   Cork

NAME THE TEAM 11

14.   Tim Howard
2.   Gary Neville
25.   John O'Shea
27.   Mikael Silvestre
6.   Wes Brown

7.	Cristiano Ronaldo
16.	Roy Keane
24.	Darren Fletcher
11.	Ryan Giggs
18.	Paul Scholes
10.	Ruud Van Nistelrooy

KEANO

1081.	Cork
1082.	Cobh Ramblers
1083.	True
1084.	Mick McCarthy
1085.	Norwich City
1086.	Nottingham Forest
1087.	£3.75million
1088.	Eric Cantona
1089.	The FA Premier League (1994)
1090.	The World Club Championship (Toyota Cup in Tokyo)

GOALKEEPERS

1091.	Alex Stepney, David Gaskell & Harry Gregg
1092.	Jimmy Rimmer
1093.	Birmingham City
1094.	Gary Walsh
1095.	Newcastle
1096.	Alex Stepney
1097.	Birmingham City
1098.	Mark Bosnich
1099.	Jimmy Rimmer
1100.	Paddy Roche

RUUD

1101.	2001
1102.	PSV Eindhoven
1103.	Den Bosch
1104.	1998
1105.	Dutch Player of the Year
1106.	2002-03
1107.	Germany
1108.	£19million
1109.	Fulham
1110.	He damaged his cruciate ligament

TRIVIA 14

| 1111. | They were all club mascots |
| 1112. | True |

1113.	Ron Atkinson
1114.	Two (the World Club Championship Trophy & The Toyota Cup)
1115.	Five (1995 Ajax Amsterdam, 1996 Juventus, 1997 Borussia Dortmund & 1998 Real Madrid)
1116.	Eric Cantona (50% of the votes)
1117.	George Best (37% of the votes)
1118.	False (the Referee pointed to the dressing rooms as Red Cards were not in regular use at the time)
1119.	True (he topped the polling)
1120.	Fourth (Bill Shankly 2nd & Brian Clough 3rd)

SEASON 2002 - 2003 - 2

1121.	Real Madrid
1122.	Portsmouth
1123.	Ruud Van Nistelrooy
1124.	Paul Scholes
1125.	Quarter-Finals
1126.	Charlton Athletic
1127.	Juventus
1128.	West Ham United
1129.	Manchester City 3 Manchester United 1
1130.	David Beckham (he signed for Real Madrid during the summer)

THE SCANDINAVIAN LINK

1131.	32
1132.	Ronny Johnsen
1133.	Bordeax & S. M. Caen
1134.	The 1997-1998 UEFA Champions League (1. FC Kosice away)
1135.	Ron Atkinson (in February 1986)
1136.	Chelsea (in the 1997 Charity Shield at Wembley)
1137.	5
1138.	False (he played in the UEFA Champions League games against Juventus & Feyenoord, but Raimond Van Der Gouw replaced him for the Coca-Cola Cup tie at Ipswich Town)
1139.	AS Saint-Etienne
1140.	John Hartson (for West Ham United at Old Trafford on 13.9.97)

SEASON 2003 - 2004 - 2

1141.	75
1142.	Paul Scholes
1143.	John O'Shea
1144.	Quinton Fortune
1145.	Leicester City
1146.	Louis Saha (versus Fulham)
1147.	Manchester City
1148.	Cristiano Ronaldo
1149.	Gary Neville

1150.   Nicky Butt (he moved to Newcastle United in the summer)

LEGEND - GEORGE BEST
1151.   1946
1152.   Belfast
1153.   West Bromwich Albion
1154.   Wales
1155.   FA Youth Cup Winners' medal (1964)
1156.   Hockey
1157.   1968
1158.   27
1159.   Fort Lauderdale Strikers & San Jose Earthquakes
1160.   37

GERMAN CONFRONTATIONS
1161.   Borussia Dortmund [European Cup, 1st Round - 1956-1957]
1162.   3-2 [3-2 to United in the home leg, 0-0 away]
1163.   2-2
1164.   Dwight Yorke & Paul Scholes
1165.   The Olympic Stadium
1166.   1972
1167.   Borussia Dortmund [Round 2]
1168.   Bixente Lizarazu
1169.   Markus Babbel
1170.   It was their 150th goal in the European Cup

LEGEND - DAVID BECKHAM
1171.   FA Youth Cup Winners' medal
1172.   Nantes
1173.   Tottenham Hotspur
1174.   The PFA Young Player of the Year
1175.   Preston North End
1176.   Galatasaray
1177.   Real Madrid (Quarter-Final at Old Trafford in April 2003)
1178.   Aston Villa ("You'll never win anything with kids" quote from Alan Hansen followed
          this game)
1179.   Chelsea
1180.   Argentina

SEASON 2000 - 2001
1181.   80
1182.   Fulham
1183.   Anderlecht, Dynamo Kiev & PSV Eindhoven
1184.   Teddy Sheringham (he re-joined Spurs at the end of the season)
1185.   Ole Gunnar Solskjaer
1186.   West Ham United

1187.   Valencia
1188.   David Beckham
1189.   Paolo Di Canio
1190.   Bayern Munich

KNIGHT OF 1,000 GAMES
1191.   Oxford United
1192.   QPR
1193.   John Sivebaek
1194.   Pecsi Munkas
1195.   Arsenal (48)
1196.   Brian McClair
1197.   Tottenham Hotspur (25)
1198.   Sir Matt Busby
1199.   Ryan Giggs
1200.   Lyon

OWEN HARGREAVES
1201.   Canada
1202.   Paraguay
1203.   Uli Hoeness
1204.   2001 (August)
1205.   Netherlands
1206.   Manchester City (a 1-0 away defeat on 19th August 2007)
1207.   2000
1208.   Calgary Foothills
1209.   26-years old
1210.   17m euros

SEASON 1999 - 2000 - 2
1211.   Everton (at Goodison Park on 8 August 1999, 1-1)
1212.   91
1213.   Southampton (away on 22 April 2000 - 3-1 win)
1214.   4
1215.   7 draws & 3 defeats
1216.   97
1217.   United did not enter the 1999-2000 competition
1218.   Chelsea, Tottenham Hotspur & Newcastle United
1219.   Southampton (away)
1220.   Dwight Yorke (Trinidad & Tobago)

THE 1999/2000 FIFA CLUB WORLD CHAMPIONSHIP
1221.   Brazil
1222.   The Maracana
1223.   3rd
1224.   Dwight Yorke

1225. Nicky Butt
1226. 1 - David Beckham (versus Rayos del Necaxa)
1227. Vasco da Gama
1228. Quinton Fortune
1229. Danny Higginbotham (David May joined Huddersfield Town on loan on 24 December 1999)
1230. Corinthians (Brazil)

MIXED BAG - 4
1231. Clausenegen FK & Molde
1232. The FA Cup in 1990
1233. Arsenal (4-2 at home & 2-1 away)
1234. Ole Gunnar Solskjaer
1235. Watford (at Vicarage Road on 29 April 2000)
1236. Reggina
1237. Football Writers' Player of the Year & the PFA Player of the Year Award
1238. False (it was a Division 1 game, the Premier League was not formed until season 1992-1993)
1239. Ruud Van Nistlerooy
1240. Robbie Fowler (Liverpool)

TRIVIA 15
1241. False, it was his fifth award
1242. Arnold Muhren (1983 v Brighton & Hove Albion)
1243. Davor Suker (Red Star Belgrade)
1244. Luis Figo
1245. AS Monaco
1246. £7.8m
1247. David Beckham, Gary Neville, Phil Neville & Paul Scholes
1248. David Beckham
1249. John Curtis
1250. Jaap Stam, Roy Keane, David Beckham & Andy Cole